C I T Y P A C K
Lisbon

By Tim Jepson

Fodor's

Fodor's Travel Publications
New York • Toronto • London • Sydney • Auckland

WWW.FODORS.COM

Contents

About this book

Citypack Lisbon is divided into six sections to cover the six most important aspects of your visit to Lisbon. It includes:

- An overview of the city and its people
- Itineraries, walks, and excursions
- The top 25 sights to visit
- Features about different aspects of the city that make it special
- Detailed listings of restaurants, hotels, stores, and nightlife
- Practical information

In addition, easy-to-read side panels provide fascinating extra facts and snippets, highlights of places to visit, and invaluable practical advice.

CROSS-REFERENCES

To help you make the most of your visit, cross-references, indicated by ➤, show you where to find additional information about a place or subject.

MAPS

The fold-out map in the wallet at the back of the book is a comprehensive street plan of Lisbon. All the map references given in the book refer to this map. For example, the Igreja de São Roque in Largo Trindado Coelho has the following information: ✚ H8; a11 indicating the grid square of the main map (H8) and the grid square (a11) of the inset central enlargement in which the Igreja de São Roque will be found.

The city-center maps found on the inside front and back covers of the book itself are for quick reference. They show the Top 25 Sights in the city, described on pages 24–48, which are clearly plotted by number (❶ – ㉕, not page number) from west to east across the city.

ADMISSION CHARGES

An indication of the admission charge (for all attractions) is given by categorizing the standard adult rate as follows: ✋ Expensive (over 700 escudos), ✋ Moderate (400–700 escudos), and ✋ Inexpensive (under 400 escudos). The '$' is placed between the escudos and the centavos, for example 700$00.

LISBON
life

INTRODUCING LISBON

The Bairro Alto, a maze of attractive old streets

Lisbon Tourist Card

The Lisbon Tourist Card (*Cartão-Card Lisboa*) gives free admittance to 25 city museums, discounts on other attractions, and free use of public transportation (except trams 15 and 28, and the Santa Justa elevator). It is valid for 24, 48, or 72 hours, and is sold at the post office at Rua Jardim do Regedor 50 (across from the main tourist office in Praça dos Restauradores), the Museu de Arte Antiga, and the Mosteiro dos Jerónimos. Children pay a reduced price. For transportation-only passes ➤ 90–91.

Lisbon's strategic position at the mouth of the River Tagus has attracted settlers and invaders alike since around 1200 BC. This geographic feature, along with a number of key historical events and figures, have been decisive in shaping the city. From its days as a "serene harbor," as it was known by the Greeks, to its zenith during the Age of Discoveries, through the dictatorships of Pombal and Salazar, it has emerged into the modern age as a flourishing European capital.

Little physical evidence remains in today's modern city of its Greek, Roman, and Visigoth invaders, but you can see the influence of four centuries of Muslim occupation (711–1147). Their hilltop palace, the Alcáçova, now the site of the Castelo São Jorge, was surrounded by a wall, remains of which still stand. Below are a labyrinth of protective narrow streets known as the *al hama* (Alfama), or "hot waters" after the spring that emerged there. On capturing Lisbon in 1147, Afonso Henriques confined any remaining Moors into the Mouraria, an area behind the castle that retains its name to this day (Mouro—Portuguese for Moor). He also built the Sé (cathedral) in 1150, much of which still stands, supposedly on the site of the Moorish mosque.

During the reign of Dom Dinis (1279–1325) Spain finally recognized Portugal's borders, universities were founded and trade was encouraged. Peace and prosperity was short lived, as by the mid-14th century bad harvests, famine, plague, economic depression, and an earthquake crippled the city. However, the Spanish, who were once again threatening the independence of this fledgling nation, were finally

defeated in 1385, paving the way for the Age of Discoveries (1415–1598). Henry the Navigator, with his insatiable thirst for geographical knowledge, accuracy, riches, and the discovery of new lands, propelled Portugal to the pinnacle of world power. Risking the Sea of Darkness, reputedly filled with monsters and serpents, the explorers opened up the world to trade, colonization, and knowledge. Lisbon became a coffer, overflowing with gold, silver, ivory, wood, and spices, as caravels returned from around the world to dock in the capital.

Lisbon's glory did not last. Wealth soon disappeared to the hands of merchants and Portugal's western sea routes were threatened by the Dutch, French, and English. Religious turmoil was rife in Europe and by 1536 the Inquisition had reached Lisbon and was to remain active until 1821. The violent earthquake that hit Lisbon in November, 1755, destroyed some 10,000 buildings and caused a total of 40,000 deaths. Ironically, it also led to the city's rebirth under the direction of the Marquês de Pombal.

The Great Earthquake

The earthquake of 1755 began at 9:30AM on November 1— All Saints' Day—when many people were at church. The effects of three tremors in ten minutes were made far worse by a tidal wave, and by fires as countless church candles were thrown over. Shock waves were felt as far away as Scotland and Jamaica. In the aftermath, corpses were sunk out at sea to halt epidemics. Taxes were suspended and prices fixed by emergency decree.

Restaurants crowd the Rua Augusta in the Baixa district

Wanting to impose order on the new Lisbon, the neo-classical buildings of the Baixa Pombalina were laid out as they stand today, on a grid plan.

Chestnut sellers by the Baixa's smart shops

Nation of tiles

Swathes of colored, patterned and painted *azulejos* (tiles) adorn many corners of Lisbon and Portugal. The first tiles were produced in 1550 for chapels, convents, and churches. With the flood of gold from Brazil in the first half of the 18th century the tiles became more ornate, while the Dutch influence and demand after the earthquake of 1755 brought more simple, cheaper tiles. By the 1760s, the tiles were being produced en masse and in the 1800s whole facades were being covered. Visit the Museu Nacional do Azulejo (▶ 48) for a visual extravaganza.

The 20th century brought more change to Portugal than any other; encompassing monarchy, republic, dictatorship, and finally parliamentary democracy. The assassination of Dom Carlos and his heir in the Praça do Comércio in 1908, effectively ended 900 years of monarchy. Liberalism, romanticism, and realism, which were flourishing among Lisbon's intellectuals, found an outlet in republicanism. Dictatorship came in 1932 in the form of António Salazar who officially preached the value of God, country, and family and whose economic genius put an end to Portugal's instability. The revolution of 1974 finally brought parliamentary democracy to Portugal and the opportunity to join the European Community. Today, instead of looking out to sea for its fortunes, Lisbon looks inland, to Europe.

This is a city still changing. Building projects abound, foreign investment rolls in, and private spending increases but Lisbon, one of Europe's smallest capitals, retains its charm and intimacy. Washing hangs from flower-filled balconies, Moorish alleys twist around dark corners, the smell of coffee wafts from the turn-of-the-century bars and Lisboetas, the Lisbon people, fill a thousand cafés and ramshackle restaurants with animated talk. Ancient trams, clanking elevators, and funiculars add to the period feel, as do the shoeshine men. This is city where you can still see the age-old chestnut vendors selling their wares from scented braziers right in the heart of the modern city.

LISBON IN FIGURES

Geography

- Latitude: 38° 43' N
- Longitude: 9° 08' W
- Same latitude as: Washington D.C., San Francisco, Ibiza, Sicily, Seoul
- Area of city: 1,066sq miles
- Proportion of Portugal's area: 3 percent
- Distance from western edge of continental Europe: 25 miles
- Number of hills: 7
- Distance from New York: 3,400 miles
- From San Francisco: 5,720 miles
- From London 1,390 miles
- From Tokyo: 6,980 miles
- From Singapore: 7,425 miles

1755 Earthquake

- Population before earthquake: 270,000
- Estimated number killed in Lisbon: 60,000
- Height of tidal wave: 41 feet
- Number of buildings destroyed: 9,000

People & City

- Population of Portugal: 10,421,000
- Proportion of Roman Catholics: 94 percent
- Population of Greater Lisbon: 2,131,000
- Population of Lisbon: 950,000
- Lisbon's literacy rate: 87 percent
- Lisbon's traffic accidents: one of Europe's highest rates. In one month in 2000, there were 3,500 accidents leading to 103 deaths
- Lisbon has more men with mustaches than any other European city, with 47 percent of Portuguese men sporting a mustache

On top of the world beside the Discovery Monument in Belém

A CHRONOLOGY

711	The Moors take control of much of Portugal, including Lisbon, and rule for over 400 years.
1139	Afonso Henriques, son of a French count and a Castilian princess, declares himself first king of "Portucale."
1147	Lisbon is captured from the Moors by Afonso Henriques after a 17-week siege, with the help of soldiers bound for the Second Crusade.
1195	St. Anthony of Padua is born in Lisbon.
1249	The loss of Faro in the Algarve marks the end of Moorish power in Portugal.
1255	King Afonso III makes Lisbon capital of Portugal in place of Coimbra.
1382	Death of King Fernado I, marking the end of the rule of the House of Burgandy.
1385	The Portuguese victory against Castile at the Battle of Aljubarrota secures Portuguese independence for some 200 years.
1419	Henry the Navigator's first square-rigged *barcas* sets out in search of a sea route to the Orient. They reach Madeira and—eight years later—the Azores.
1498	Four ships under Vasco da Gama leave Lisbon and pioneer a sea route to the East Indies, thus breaking the monopoly of Venetian and Ottoman traders in the East.
1500	Pedro Álvares Cabral "discovers" Brazil, whose riches help make Portugal the wealthiest country in Europe.
1580	A crisis in the Portuguese succession allows Philip II of Spain to invade Portugal and declare himself Philip I of Portugal.
1640	The Spanish are overthrown and replaced by the Bragança dynasty of Portuguese kings.

1755 | On November 1 two-thirds of the city is destroyed by the Great Earthquake; Dom José I is on the throne. Lisbon's reconstruction along a grid plan is masterminded by the Marquês de Pombal.

1777 | Dom José dies, Pombal is dismissed, and his rule of despotism ends. Dona Maria I takes the throne.

1807 | Portugal refuses to join Napoleon's naval blockade of Britain, its ally, and is attacked by a French army under General Junot.

1810 | During the ensuing Peninsular Wars, the Duke of Wellington builds the fortifications known as the Lines of Torres Vedras to protect Lisbon.

1834 | Marks end of the "War of the Two Brothers" between Dom Pedro IV, emperor of Brazil, and Dom Miguel for Portuguese succession.

1908 | King Carlos I and his eldest son, Luis Filipe, are assassinated in the Praça do Comércio.

1910 | The Portuguese monarchy is overthrown and replaced by a republic. Dona Amélia and her son King Manuel II are exiled to England.

1932 | Dr. António de Oliveira Salazar is made Prime Minister and rules as a dictator until 1968.

1974 | The Carnation Revolution of April 25 ends some 40 years of dictatorship.

1983 | Mario Soars of the Socialist Party is elected Prime Minister, becoming President in 1991.

1986 | Portugal joins the European Community.

1988 | Violent fire destroys a large part of Lisbon's old Chiado district.

1995 | Jorge Sampaio elected President.

1998 | Lisbon hosts Expo '98—universal exposition.

2004 | Portugal to host Euro 2004 soccer European championship.

People & Events from History

Monument to the Marquês de Pombal

Literary genius

José Maria Eça de Queiroz (1845–1900) was one of the pre-eminent members of the so-called "Geraçap dos Setena" (generations of the seventies), a group of Lisbon essayists, idealists, and philosophers who paved the way for the political changes of the 20th century. He was also a luminary of Portuguese literature. A master of prose whose characters are alive and vibrant and plots filled with suspense, tension, and humor; his style gives a critical portrayal of upper-class life in the 19th century. Works include *Cousin Basilio* and *The Maias*.

HENRY THE NAVIGATOR

Ironically, Henry the Navigator, the driving force behind Portugal's "Age of Discovery," never traveled further than Morocco, but dedicated himself to exploration and maritime research from his Sagres promontory. Surrounding himself with the best charts, manuals, cartographers, and sailors, his dream was to discover a route to the Indies. Fighting superstition and fear of the unknown, Maderia, the Azores, and west Africa were all discovered before his death in 1460.

MARQUÊS DE POMBAL

The Marquês de Pombal, King José I's powerful First Minister, is associated with cruelty, repression, and reform. He is famous for rebuilding the city after the Great Earthquake that still characterizes the city's Baixa district. He reorganized education, bureaucracy, and trading practices, expelled the Jesuits, and stripped the feared Inquisition of its powers. Slavery was abolished, noble privileges were reduced, but dissenters were ruthlessly repressed. His power declined on the accession of Maria I in 1777.

SALAZAR

Salazar, the dictator who ruled Portugal from 1928 until 1968, was born in 1889. Graduating in law from Coimbra University, he became a professor of economics. In 1928, Portugal's economy was in tatters, Salazar became Finance Minister, a post he accepted on condition that he be given full control over spending. Within a year, he had balanced the books (they remained balanced until 1974), and within five years had made himself indispensable. Financial omnipotence soon allowed him to take control of most other areas of Portuguese life. Censorship in his Estado Novo, or New State, was absolute and education was strictly controlled. Secret police and informers proliferated. A stroke in 1968 eventually deprived the dictator of power, but his repressive regime endured until the 1974 Carnation Revolution, the peaceful revolution in which soldiers put carnations down the gun barrels.

LISBON
how to organize your time

ITINERARIES

Most of Lisbon's sightseeing highlights are in convenient clusters in different districts. The main exceptions are the Museu Calouste Gulbenkian, the Museu Nacional de Arte Antiga, the Museu do Azulejo, and the sights at Belém, but all of these are easy to reach by public transportation. You can also take a train to Sintra (► 20), but you need to rent a car, take a taxi or join a tour to see all its sights. If you have time, consider staying at Sintra overnight.

Some of the older districts of Lisbon, such as the Alfama (► 16, 44), have many side streets and alleys making unplanned wandering also rewarding.

ITINERARY ONE	THE ROSSIO AND THE OLD CITY
Morning	Start at Praça dos Restauradores. Visit the tourist office in the Palácio Foz on the west side of the square (► 90). Walk south into Praça Dom Pedro IV, better known as the Rossio (► 39), passing the handsome Rossio railroad station. Walk through the Baixa on Rua Augusta (► 40). Praça do Comércio (► 41) Sé (► 42) Museu das Artes Decorativas (► 45).
Lunch	Try the pleasant café of the Museu das Artes Decorativas; a snack or light meal from a bar on the approach to the Castelo (► 16, Walk); or consider a picnic in the delightful Castelo gardens (► 43).
Afternoon	Castelo de São Jorge (► 43) Museu da Marioneta (► 51) Igreja de São Vicente de Fora (► 55) Campo de Santa Clara (► 46) Igreja de Santa Engrácia (► 54) Museu Nacional Militar (► 52) Alfama (► 44).
ITINERARY TWO	MUSEUMS AND ART GALLERIES
Morning	Take the Metro (subway) from the Rossio or Praça dos Restauradores to São Sebastião and spend the morning visiting the treasures of the Museu Calouste Gulbenkian (► 33) and the Centro de Arte Moderna (► 34) Return by Metro to Restauradores.

Afternoon   Explore the Chiado (➤ 37, ➤ 17). Walk or take the Elevador da Glória from the Praça dos Restauradores. Catch a bird's-eye view of Lisbon from the Miradouro de São Pedro (➤ 53), then visit Igreja de São Roque (➤ 36) and Museu Arqueológico do Carmo (➤ 38). Take tram 28 to the Basílica da Estrela (➤ 32); or walk to Rua do Arsenal for a bus to the Museu Nacional de Arte Antiga (➤ 31).

ITINERARY THREE   BELÉM

Morning   Start at the Rossio, and walk through the Baixa to Rua do Arsenal-Praça do Comércio. Catch tram 15 or bus 28 or 43 along the waterfront to Belém, a short ride from central Lisbon. Spend the day visiting Belém's historic buildings.
Mosteiro dos Jerónimos (➤ 28)
Padrão dos Descobrimentos (➤ 27)
Torre de Belém (➤ 24)
Museu de Arte Popular (➤ 50)
Museu de Marinha (➤ 25).

Lunch   Buy a snack preferably from the café and patisserie Antiga Casa dos Pastéis (➤ 69). Or eat at one of the restaurants on the main Rua de Belém or Rua Vieira Portuense, one block south.

Afternoon   Museu Nacional de Arqueologia (➤ 26)
Museu Nacional dos Coches (➤ 29)
Return to city center by bus or tram.

ITINERARY FOUR   EAST LISBON

Morning   Make the trip out to the Igreja da Madre de Deus (➤ 47) and the Museu Nacional do Azulejo (➤ 48), both of which have cafés.

Afternoon   Catch a bus (28, 82) out to the Parque das Nações and visit the oceanarium (➤ 60), and Vasco da Gama tower (➤ 60) or the Lisbon Cable Car (➤ 60) for excellent views of the city. Take a walk around Lisbon's newest shopping mall, the Vasco da Gama (➤ 70) and then catch the Metro back to town.

WALKS

BAIXA, CASTELO, AND ALFAMA

Head south from Praça dos Restauradores. Note the lovely old facade of the Rossio railroad station on your right (Praça João da Câmara). Walk down the Rossio, Lisbon's main square, and then pick up Rua Augusta, a pedestrian-only street through the Baixa.

At the end look at the Praça do Comércio. Then go back to the Baixa and turn right on Rua da Conceição, crossing Largo da Madalena. Climb to the Sé (cathedral). Then follow the street uphill to the left of the cathedral.

Continue to Santa Luzia and its viewpoint (*miradouro*). Cross the road to see the Museu das Artes Decorativas (Decorative Arts Museum). As you leave the museum, turn right (the way you came) and take the first right (Travessa de Santa Luzia) and continue uphill (bearing right), following the yellow signs to the Castelo de São Jorge.

Walk the length of the walkway under the castle walls, emerging through a green iron gate to Largo do Menino de Deus (down to your left). Turn left onto the shabby square and find Rua da Santa Marinha at its top (north) side. Follow to São Vicente de Fora church.

Flower stall in the Baixa's Rua Augusta

Take the street to the left of the church to Campo de Santa Clara. Walk towards the small garden and palm trees, then drop right to come around behind the church of Santa Engrácia. With your back to the facade, go left down past the brown-tiled house ahead. Turn right on Rua dos Remédios at the bottom.

Detour south to visit the Museu Nacional Militar, or turn right to Rua São Estêvão and then turn left to pick up the atmospheric Rua São Miguel. Return to the cathedral on Rua de São João de Praça, and go back to the Baixa.

INFORMATION

Distance 2 miles
Time 2–3 hours depending on
   visits
Start point Praça dos
   Restauradores
🚇 H7; all
🚋 Restauradores
End point Baixa
🚇 J8; bIII
🚋 Baixa-Chiado

CHIADO SHOPPING STREETS

This is not a long walk, but it can be extended to take in the streets of the Bairro Alto to the north and west. However, the character of the two adjoining districts is very different, and in the Bairro Alto—where the streets are like a maze—it is difficult to follow any set itinerary.

Begin in the Rossio and take the pedestrian-only Rua do Carmo uphill. On your left you pass the Elevador de Santa Justa, built in 1902 and often wrongly attributed to Gustav Eiffel (it was designed by Raul Mésnier, one of his pupils).

Turn right onto Rua Garrett, the Chiado's most prestigious street. Walk to the top and note the statue of poet Fernando Pessoa and the splendid old Café A Brasileira to its right. A few doors to the right on the same side of the street is the equally revered Pastelaria Benard.

Café A Brasileira in the Rua Garrett

Turn back down Rua Garrett a few steps and look into the Igreja dos Mártires, a church erected over a 12th-century burial ground and camp of the Crusaders during the siege of Lisbon. Take Rua Serpa Pinto to the right of the church and walk down past the Teatro São Carlos and hospital.

Visit the Museu do Chiado, then continue to the bottom of the street. Turn right and then first right to double back up to Rua Garrett. Turn left onto the square, right up Rua da Misericórdia, and first right at Largo da Trindade. Then turn right and left to follow Rua da Trindade to the shady Largo do Carmo.

Visit the ruined Carmo church and museum. Then follow Rua da Oliveira northeast and turn right down the steps, noticing the narrow view of the Baixa and Castelo. Follow the steps down past the station and cross Rua 1 de Dezembro to return to the Rossio.

THE SIGHTS

INFORMATION

Distance 1 mile
Time 2 hours with visits
Start/End point Rossio

🚇 Rossio

🚌 H8; bIII

EVENING STROLLS

INFORMATION

Distance About 580 yards
Time 20 minutes
Start point Praça do Comércio
✚ J8; bIV
🚌 Services to Praça do Comércio
End point Café A Brasileira, Rua Garrett 120
✚ H8; all

Start your stroll in the Praça do Comércio

BAIXA AND CHIADO

In a perfect world, the nicest place for an evening stroll in Lisbon would be the atmospheric streets and alleys of the old Alfama district. Sadly, the increasing amount of petty crime here means it is an area best avoided after dark. This leaves the busier Baixa and Chiado quarters as the best bet for a short pre-dinner stroll. Start on the waterfront in the Praça do Comércio and then walk north on Rua Augusta (or any other of the Baixa's grid of north-running streets). Turn left onto Rua de Santa Justa, and

at its end ride the Santa Justa elevator (note the views) to the Largo do Carmo. From this little square, walk south to Rua Garrett. Turn right onto this street and walk to the Café A Brasileira (► 69), a lovely old-fashioned place for a pre-dinner drink.

BAIRRO ALTO

The Bairro Alto is one of the city's principal nightlife areas, and a pleasant place for a stroll before you eat in one of its many restaurants, or try out its bars. As with many old city quarters its streets are a tightly woven web which does not lend itself to fixed itineraries. Unplanned wandering is more fun. The best place to start is the Largo do Chiado on the area's western fringe. From there you should head northwest to the grid of streets above Rua de Loreto. Most of the restaurants, bars, and clubs are concentrated here, dotted around streets such as Travessa do Paço da Cidade and Rua do Diário de Notícias. Aim to finish with a glass of port at the Solar do Vinho do Porto, the bar run by the Port Wine Institute (► panel 78).

INFORMATION

Distance About 450 yards
Time About 10 minutes
Start point Largo do Chiado
✚ H8; alll
🚌 58,100; tram 28
End point Solar do Vinho do Porto, Rua de São Pedro de Alcântara 45 R/C
✚ H8; all
🚌 58, 100

ORGANIZED SIGHTSEEING

TRAM RIDES
Trams are an inexpensive and fun way of seeing the city. Tram 28 runs from the Church of São Vicente in the east to the Jardim da Estrela in the west, via the Baixa. Other good routes include the 12 from São Tomé in the Alfama district to Largo Martim Moniz, and the 15 or 18 (except Sundays) along the waterfront from Praça do Comércio to Belém. In summer, there are usually two tourist tram routes: the Circuito Colinas, or Hills Circuit, and the Circuito Tejo, or River Tagus Circuit. Ask at the tourist office or Carris bus ☎ 213 632 044

Hop on a tram to explore the old city

RIVER TOURS
Several companies run trips on the River Tagus, mostly between April and October. Some run by day, others by night. A few offer mini-cruises (contact tourist office), taking up to seven hours to run up and down the Cascais coast to the west of the city. For shorter trips, go to the quays on the Praça do Comércio, from where many tour boats and ferries depart (► 59). For two-hour river cruises, contact the tourist office or Cruzeiros no Tejo ☎ 218 820 348

GRAY LINE
Gray Line offer a five-hour tour of all the city's main sights, including those in the out-lying suburb of Belém. There are two departures daily (morning and afternoon) all year round, and the cost is about 5,000$00. Also available are a full-day tour of Lisbon and the Costa Azul (one a day: Apr–Oct: Mon–Fri; Nov–Mar: Tue, Thu; costing around 12,000$00); a "Lisbon by Night" tour (three times weekly year round, 12,000$00); the Costa do Estoril and Sintra (one daily year round, 8,500$00); and three-day coach trips across Portugal from Lisbon. They also offer a mini-cruise and longer trips by boat to Coimbra, Évora, Mafra, and Óbidos ☎ 213 522 594/213 560 668

Other established companies offering a wide variety of tours include Portugal Tours ☎ 213 522 902 and Cityrama ☎ 213 558 564; info@cityrama.pt

Finding tours
Details of tours and tour companies can be found in travel agencies, the lobbies of most major hotels, and the main city tourist office in Praça dos Restauradores. Organized tours are the easiest way to visit Sintra (► 20), whose palaces and gardens are dispersed over a wide area. Most companies make scheduled pick-ups at the city's leading hotels.

EXCURSIONS

INFORMATION

Sintra
Distance 15 miles
Journey time 45 minutes by train
🚆 Trains about every 20 minutes
from Lisbon's Estação Rossio
ℹ️ Praça da República 23
☎ 219 231 157

Palácio Nacional de Sintra
✉️ Largo da Rainha D Amélia,
Sintra-Vila
☎ 219 106 840
🕐 Tue–Thu 10–5
🎟️ Summer: moderate; winter:
inexpensive

Castelo dos Mouros
✉️ Calçada dos Clérigos
☎ None
🕐 Jun–Sep: daily 10–6.
Oct–Mar: daily 10–5
🎟️ Free

Palácio Nacional da Pena
✉️ Estrada da Pena
☎ 219 105 340
🕐 Palace Jun–Sep: Tue–Sun
10–6. May–Oct: 10–5. Park
Jun–Sep: daily10–6.
Oct–May: 10–5
🎟️ Moderate

Palácio de Monserrate
✉️ Estrada de Monserrate
☎ 219 247 200
🕐 Gardens only: daily 10–5,
last entry 4
🎟️ Free

SINTRA

Many excursions are possible from Lisbon—visits by rail to the nearby beach towns of Estoril and Cascais, for example, are summer favorites—but none are as popular as the trip to Sintra, a town of sumptuous royal palaces and beautiful landscapes some 15 miles from the capital. Sintra is not a single sight, however, and can be disorientating. You will need to use taxis or rent a car to move between the various sights, or join an organized tour (➤ 19), as buses are irregular.

In Sintra-Vila (the town itself) the main thing to see is the Palácio Nacional, begun by Dom João I in the 15th century and used as a royal palace until the end of the 19th century. It has lavishly decorated state rooms and many beautiful tiles.

Just south of Sintra-Vila lies the Castelo dos Mouros, a Moorish castle begun in the 8th century and captured by Afonso Henriques in 1147. The views from its rocky pinnacles are magnificent. Further south, around 2 miles from Sintra-Vila, lies another royal palace, the Palácio da Pena, a wonderfully pretentious monument built in the 19th century by Ferdinand of Saxe-Coburg-Gotha, the husband of Queen Maria II.

The Palácio Nacional in Sintra-Vila

A madcap medieval pastiche, its exterior is all battlements and bristling towers. Inside is a profusion of hangings, heavy furniture, extravagant stucco, and excessive decorative flourishes. Its park and gardens are delightful, and the views from its terraces sublime. If you want still better panoramas, try the nearby Cruz Alta (1,400 feet), the highest point in the Serra de Sintra hills.

Pena's gardens, like much of the countryside around Sintra, are beautifully verdant—a "glorious Eden" in the words of Lord Byron. Better still are the gardens of the Palácio de Monserrate, a pastoral idyll 2.5 miles west of Sintra. William Beckford, a wealthy English exile, added an English garden here in 1793.

Another must is the recently restored Quinta da Regaleira, one of the finest examples of turn of the 20th century revivalist art, with its masonic "well of initiation," gargoyles, mythological grottos, and neo-Manueline palace and chapel. The palace was built just to the east of Sintra by its owner Carralho Monteiro (1850–1920) in conjunction with the Italian architect Luigi Manini (1848–1936).

MAFRA

Mafra, a little town 25 miles northwest of Lisbon, is dominated by the Palácio Nacional de Mafra, one of the largest baroque monasteries, and palaces in Europe. Begun in 1717, it was built by Dom João V, who six years earlier had pledged to build a monastery should he and his wife have a child. Bárbara, the future Queen of Spain, was born within a year. Finance for the project was provided by the gold and diamonds of Brazil. Initially the plan was for a monastery of 13 monks. In the end it housed 300. Around 50,000 laborers and 7,000 soldiers worked on the building, a huge folly of 2,500 windows, 5,200 doors, and 880 rooms, which took 13 years to build. Today you can view the rather chill church and many of the rooms.

INFORMATION

Sintra (continued)

Quinta da Regaleira
- ✉ Qunita da Regaleira, Sintra
- ☎ 219 106 650, call to reserve tour and for tour times
- 🎟 Expensive

A statue-lined corridor of the Palácio de Mafra

Mafra
Distance 25 miles
Journey time 90 minutes by bus

Palácio Nacional de Mafra
- ☎ 261 810 550
- 🕐 Wed–Mon 10–4:45. Guided tours last an hour
- 🚌 Empresa Mafrense buses depart hourly from Largo Martin Moniz, northeast of the Rossio in Lisbon
- 🎟 Summer: moderate; winter: inexpensive
- ❓ Organized sightseeing tours often include Mafra (► 19)

What's On

February/March *Carnival celebrations*: Parades, parties, and fancy dress take place around the city before Lent (date depends on when Easter falls).

March/April *Calvary procession*: Through the Graça district on Good Friday. Easter celebrations throughout the city.

April *Carnation Revolution*: Celebrations to commemorate April 25, 1974, when soldiers put flowers in the barrels of their guns. The bull-fighting season starts at Campo Pequeno, and continues until October.

May *Annual book fair*: Held for three weeks in the Parque Eduardo VII. The first annual pilgrimage to Fátima, the most important in Portugal, takes place on May 13.

June *Major feast days*: June 13 (St. Antony); June 24 (St. John); and June 29 (St. Peter). The *Festas dos Santos* (Festivals of the Saints) take place on and around these three days. *Sintra Festival*: Classical music played in Sintra's churches and palaces (June and July). *Flea market*: junk, antiques and handicrafts stalls at Sintra (June 29).

July *International summer jazz festival*: Organized by the Calouste Gulbenkian Foundation. *Festa de Colete Encarnado* ("Red Waistcoat Fair") in Vila Franca da Xira, 19 miles from Lisbon, with folk events and a bull-run through the streets (several days in the first two weeks of July). A similar event, the *Feira de Outubro*, takes place in the first two weeks of October.

August *Handicrafts fair*: Held in Cascais and Estoril.

September *Opera season*: Starts at the Teatro Nacional de São Carlos and runs to June. Also the start of the soccer season.

October *Pilgrimage*: The second of the two annual pilgrimages to Fátima takes place on October 13.

LISBON's
top 25 sights

The sights are shown on the maps on the inside front cover and inside back cover, numbered **1–25** from west to east across the city

TORRE DE BELÉM

DID YOU KNOW?

- The Torre de Belém was declared a World Heritage Site by the United Nations in 1983

INFORMATION

- B10
- Avenida de Brasília
- 213 620 034
- Tue–Sun 10–5. Closed public hols
- 27, 28, 29, 43, 49, 51; tram 15
- Belém (Cascais line) from Cais do Sodré
- Very poor
- Moderate. Free on Sun and public hols until 2
- Museu de Marinha (➤ 25), Museu Nacional de Arqueologia (➤ 26), Padrão dos Descobrimentos (➤ 27), Mosteiro dos Jerónimos (➤ 28), Museu Nacional dos Coches (➤ 29)

Delicate stonework on the Torre de Belém

Few buildings are as charming or evocative as the Torre de Belém, a capricious architectural confection of towers, turrets, and battlements, whose tawny-colored ramparts are washed by the River Tagus on three sides.

National landmark Lisbon's Belém tower is not only a masterpiece of Renaissance and Manueline architecture, but also one of Portugal's most potent national symbols. A monument to the country's maritime triumphs across the centuries, it was built between 1515 and 1520 by Francisco de Arruda, a Portuguese architect who had previously worked on a variety of military projects in Morocco. His travels in North Africa made a lasting impression on him, and this is reflected in the use of a wide range of Moorish motifs on the tower. Chief of these are the little domes crowning the battlements, and the jutting corner sentry boxes, which are combined with arcaded windows and delicate Venetian-style loggias.

Changing roles Once the tower stood proudly out in the river, acting as a defensive bastion guarding the Restelo, or harbor, from pirates. Today the Tagus's ever-changing course has left it stranded on the shore. Close to, you can make out the cross motif adorning every battlement. This was the symbol of the Order of Christ, the successor to the Knights Templar in Portugal. A jutting bastion leads to a small internal cloister, below which are rudimentary storerooms and dungeons (the tower served as a prison from 1580 to 1828). The breezy second-story terrace —which gives good views—features an intricately carved statue of the Madonna (Our Lady of the Safe Homecoming). Steps lead up to the top of the tower for more views.

MUSEU DE MARINHA

Even if you don't normally rate boats and the sea, Lisbon's excellent maritime museum is irresistible. It is one of the most important of its kind in Europe, and fully captures the splendor of Portugal's long and distinguished history of seafaring.

Seafaring nation It seems only right that Lisbon's maritime museum should be housed in Belém, for it was from the sheltered harbor nearby that many of the great Portuguese explorers embarked on their voyages of discovery. Today the museum occupies both the west wing of the Mosteiro dos Jerónimos, and part of the nearby Galeotas Pavilion. The former is home to a collection of model boats and other maritime ephemera, the latter to full-size craft, planes, and several impressive royal barges. There is also a children's museum, the Museu das Crianças.

Maritime History The bulk of the museum's more venerable exhibits were provided by a private bequest in 1948. So many items were lost or destroyed in the 1755 earthquake that it was not easy to find early artifacts for the museum. Much of the collection proceeds chronologically, from the era of the Great Discoveries onwards. The oldest exhibit is a wooden figure representing the Archangel Raphael, which accompanied Vasco da Gama on his pioneering voyage to the Indies in 1497. From the 19th century comes the ornate splendor of royal yachts, including a reconstruction of a sumptuous cabin from the *Amélia*, built for Carlos I. There is also a section devoted to the Orient as well as model boats, maritime paintings, naval uniforms, and plenty of decorated prows, maps, and navigational instruments.

HIGHLIGHTS

- State barges (Pavilhão das Galeotas)
- Model boats
- Statue of Archangel Raphael
- Cabins of the *Amélia*
- Paintings
- Prows
- Maps

INFORMATION

- ✚ B9
- ✉ Praça do Império
- ☎ 213 620 019
- ◷ Mid-June–end Sep: Tue–Sun 10–6. Early Oct–mid-June: Tue–Sun 10–5. Closed public hols
- 🚃 27, 28, 29, 43, 49, 51; tram 15
- 🚉 Belém (Cascais line) from Cais do Sodré
- ♿ Very good
- 🎟 Moderate
- ↔ Museu Nacional de Arqueologia (➤ 26), Mosteiro dos Jerónimos (➤ 28), Padrão dos Descobrimentos (➤ 27), Torre de Belém (➤ 24), Museu Nacional dos Coches (➤ 29)
- 🛈 Entrance at western end of the Mosteiro dos Jerónimos

Wooden figure of the Archangel Raphael

MUSEU NACIONAL DE ARQUEOLOGIA

HIGHLIGHTS

- Funerary monuments
- Granite boars
- Early pottery
- Roman mosaics
- Sarcophagi
- Jewelry
- Treasury

INFORMATION

- C9
- Praça do Império
- 213 620 000/213 620 022
- Wed–Sun 10–6; Tue 2–6. Closed public hols
- 17, 27, 28, 29, 43, 49, 51; tram 15
- Belém (Cascais line) from Cais do Sodré
- Good
- Moderate. Free Sun until 2
- Museu de Marinha (➤ 25), Torre de Belém (➤ 24), Padrão dos Descobrimentos (➤ 27), Mosteiro dos Jerónimos (➤ 28), Museu Nacional dos Coches (➤ 29)
- Entrance midway along the main façade of the Mosteiro dos Jerónimos

You wouldn't say this rambling archeological museum is Europe's best—in fact it is a little threadbare in places—but there are plenty of fascinating artifacts from widely differing epochs of Portuguese history to make a visit worthwhile.

Look back in time Since its foundation in 1893, the National Archeology Museum has been housed in the east wing of the Mosteiro dos Jerónimos, making it easy to visit in conjunction with the monastery church and the Museu de Marinha in the adjoining west wing. The collection includes a mixture of archeological and ethnographical items, including folk objects and religious artifacts illustrating Portugal's broader history, from the Neolithic (the late Stone Age) onwards. Earthenware pottery and funerary headstones make up the bulk of the Neolithic remains, while the Iron Age section includes the strange granite monoliths known as *berrões*, or boars that are common in many parts of northeast Portugal.

Highlights The museum becomes really enthralling in the Roman section, which has mosaics, statues, and embellished sarcophagi gathered from sites across Portugal. These offer some of the collection's most eye-catching sights. Look out in particular for the bronze figurine representing Fortune, and the Quadriga, a sculptural group of four horses pulling a chariot. Other sections are devoted to African artifacts, Egyptian pieces in particular, and to items garnered from Portugal's overseas empire or brought back by Portuguese traders. Some of the museum's loveliest exhibits are to be found in the treasury, where you can see an amazing range of Celtic earrings, bracelets, rings, and other intricately worked jewelry.

Bronze figurine of Fortune, 1st century AD

PADRÃO DOS DESCOBRIMENTOS

It must have taken courage to impose a vast modern monument on an area as historical as Belém, but this huge white waterfront edifice provides a dramatic and dignified counterpart to the venerable Torre de Belém nearby.

Maritime pride The Monument to the Discoveries was erected in 1960 during the Salazar dictatorship. It marked the 500th anniversary of the death of Henry the Navigator, the prince who laid the foundation of Portugal's wide-reaching empire through his energetic backing of projects such as a maritime school in the Algarve. The monument has been criticized for its vaguely fascist design and obviously nationalist intent, but it is nonetheless an architectural triumph, imposing itself on the Belém waterfront. Its jutting triangular pediment represents the prow of a ship, while the trio of curving forms above symbolizes billowing sails. Rising over these is a redoubtable blockhouse tower, reaching some 140 feet above the waterside.

Figures The monument's rigid lines are softened by a group of sculpted figures crowded on the pediment's sloping prow. Behind Henry, who holds a ship in his hands, stands Manuel I, the king who reigned from 1495 to 1521, during the height of Portugal's voyages of discovery. He is shown holding an armillary sphere, one of his regal symbols. Other characters include Luís de Camões (➤ 73), one of Portugal's most famous poets, who is depicted holding verses. An elevator runs to the top of the monument, from where you can look down on a mosaic map depicting the voyages of discovery.

Top: mosaic map. Below: Henry leads pediment statues

5

MOSTEIRO DOS JERÓNIMOS

DID YOU KNOW?

- The monastery was declared a World Heritage Site by the United Nations in 1983

HIGHLIGHTS

- South door
- West door
- Fan vaulting
- Nave
- Monument to Vasco da Gama
- Transept star vaulting
- Choir stalls

INFORMATION

- ✚ C9
- ✉ Praça do Império
- ☎ 213 620 034
- 🕐 Tue–Sun 10–5
- 🚌 27, 28, 29, 43, 49, 51; tram 15
- 🚆 Belém (Cascais line) from Cais do Sodré
- ♿ Poor
- 🎫 Moderate. Free Sun and public hols until 2
- ↔ Museu Nacional de Arqueologia (➤ 26), Museu de Marinha (➤ 25), Padrão dos Descobrimentos (➤ 27), Museu Nacional dos Coches (➤ 29), Torre de Belém (➤ 24)
- ❓ Tram 15 stops outside the monastery. The return stop is 135 yards east, opposite Casa dos Pastéis

It is hard to think of any greater buildings in Lisbon than those of the Mosteiro dos Jerónimos, a glorious monastic complex whose carved stonework and magnificent cloisters rival Europe's finest Gothic and Renaissance work.

Praising the explorers The present monastery is built over the site of a small chapel raised by Henry the Navigator in 1460 to offer spiritual solace to the many seafarers who embarked at Belém for their voyages of discovery. The new church was begun by Manuel I in 1502 to celebrate Vasco da Gama's successful voyage to the Indies, da Gama having held a vigil in Henry's chapel prior to his 1497 expedition. Some 50 years were to elapse before the building was completed, and during this time several architects worked on the project, hence the Gothic, Manueline, and Renaissance mixture of the church's artistic and architectural styles.

Treasures The monastery's treasures begin with the magnificent south door, whose wealth of decoration centers on the figure of Henry the Navigator (above the arch), and the contrasting west door, where the protagonists are Manuel I, his wife, Dona Maria, and the pair's respective patron saints. Inside are soaring aisles and a vast, breathtaking array of carved stone, reaching a climax in the huge sweep of fan vaulting over the nave. Take time to search out da Gama's tomb, located beneath a gallery near the church's entrance, and then make for the adjoining cloisters, one of Portugal's great architectural set-pieces. The two-story ensemble, and the lower tier in particular, is a feast of outstanding carving, the pillars and vaults embellished with a wealth of intricately sculpted stone, whose delicacy belies its strength and weight.

MUSEU NACIONAL DOS COCHES

To believe that a coach museum could be Lisbon's most visited sight is a difficult concept until you go for yourself. Then you see the sheer splendor—not to mention sheer number—of its beautifully embellished coaches and carriages.

Travel in style Lisbon's National Coach Museum is one of the best collections of its type in the world. For the Portuguese royalty and aristocracy, coaches and carriages were never merely modes of transportation, but were used to proclaim the wealth and taste of their owners. As a result, many were painted, gilded, and decorated to a magnificent degree, particularly those used for state or ceremonial occasions. The museum, founded by Queen Amélia in 1904, is housed in the former riding academy and stables of the Palácio do Belém, a royal palace begun around 1726 by Dom João V. Today the palace proper, which is closed to visitors, is the official residence of the Portuguese president.

Rich collection Three of the museum's most splendid coaches are those built in 1716 for the Marquês de Frontes, Portugal's ambassador to Pope Clement XI and the Holy See. Constructed in Italy, the coaches are decorated with allegorical scenes representing Portuguese military and maritime triumphs. Other highlights include many cabs, prams, and sedans; the royal carriage of Dom José I; a miniature carriage built for King Carlos I as a child; and the berlin made for Dona Maria I for the opening of the Basilica da Estrela. If the museum has a fault, it is that there are just too many coaches, the endless repetition dulling the wonderful impression created by the first displays.

HIGHLIGHTS

- Painted ceiling vaults
- Coaches of the Marquês de Frontes
- Dom João V's state coach
- Dom José I's state coach
- King Carlo I's miniature carriage
- Dona Maria I's royal carriage

Detail on coach

INFORMATION

- ✛ C9
- ✉ Praça Afonso de Albuquerque
- ☎ 213 610 850
- 🕐 Tue–Sun 10–6; last visit 5:30. Closed public hols
- 🚌 27, 28, 29, 43, 49, 51; tram 15
- 🚆 Belém (Cascais line) from Cais do Sodré
- ♿ Poor
- 💷 Moderate
- ↔ Mosteiro dos Jerónimos (➤ 28), Padrão dos Descobrimentos (➤ 27)

PALÁCIO DOS MARQUÊSES DE FRONTEIRA

HIGHLIGHTS

- Battle Room
- Delft, or Dining, Room
- Gallery of Arts (tiled terrace)
- Chapel
- Gardens
- Doze de Inglaterra
- Statues of the Nine Muses
- Statues of Portugal's first 15 kings

INFORMATION

- ✚ E5
- ✉ Largo de São Domingos de Benfica 1
- ☎ 217 782 023
- ◷ Palace guided tours Jun–Sep: Mon–Sat 10:30, 11, 11:30 and noon. Oct–May: Mon–Sat 11 and noon
- ◴ Sete Rios
- ▤ 72
- ♿ Poor
- ▣ Gardens moderate. Palace and gardens expensive. Admission more expensive on Sat
- ❓ Gardens not included in tour when it is raining. Opening times change regularly: call for latest details. The palace can only be visited on an official tour at the specified times. English tours available

Top: picture tiles in the gardens of the Fronteira Palace

Even if you are usually a little lazy when it comes to trekking out to the suburbs of a city to see something, the beautiful Italianate gardens and captivating tiles make the journey to the Fronteira Palace more than worthwhile.

Isolated beauty A train or subway ride from the Rossio drops you close to the Fronteira Palace in an area of somewhat moribund modern housing and half-finished roads. The palace and its gardens, an oasis of beauty in this wasteland, were founded in 1670 as a hunting lodge by João Mascarenhas, the first Marquês de Fronteira. The palace is still privately owned, but guided tours conduct you around some half-dozen rooms, notably the Battle Room, whose tiled decoration depicts scenes from the War of Restoration. This campaign brought to an end 60 years of Spanish domination in Portugal between 1581 and 1640. Fronteira was a general, and played a prominent part in the war.

Gardens The palace's Italianate gardens, full of fountains, topiary terraces, little lakes, and a dense green web of clipped hedging, are a delight, not least because of the *azulejos*, or tiles, which decorate virtually every suitable surface. You will already have seen a wide variety of tiles in the palace, including some of the first Delft tiles imported into Portugal (in the 17th century). In the gardens, there are benches, walls, and ornamental pools swathed with tiles depicting all manner of subjects—the months of the year, the planets, the signs of the zodiac and many more. The most eye-catching are the life-size depictions of the Doze de Inglaterra, 12 gallant horsemen who, according to the legend, sailed to England to fight for the honor of 12 damsels in distress.

MUSEU NACIONAL DE ARTE ANTIGA

Lisbon may have few internationally acclaimed galleries, but in this wonderful museum—not to mention the Gulbenkian Museum—the city has a gallery that stands comparison with almost any throughout Europe.

Collection The National Museum of Ancient Art contains one of Portugal's finest art collections, and ranks second only to the Gulbenkian among Lisbon's galleries and museums. The collection of paintings shows the development of Portuguese art from about the 11th century onwards, and also includes work by several of Europe's greatest artists. There is a wealth of decorative art and silverware, notably Italian ceramics, ecclesiastical vestments, Flemish tapestries, and a monstrance from the Mosteiro in Belém, reputedly made from the first gold brought back from the Indies by Vasco da Gama. Also worth seeing are a decorated chapel, preserved from a convent previously on the site, and the Namban screens, which depict the arrival of the Portuguese in Japan in 1543.

Adoration The museum's most famous painting by far is an altarpiece, the *Painéis de São Vicente de Fora*, or *Adoration of St. Vincent*, probably painted by Nuno Gonçalves between 1465 and 1470. The work was discovered only in 1882, dirty and dismembered in a defunct Lisbon church. Its six panels portray around 60 figures paying homage to St. Vincent, Lisbon's patron saint, who is depicted twice. Other treasures include works by Grão Vasco, Frei Carlos Memling, Holbein, Dürer, Raphael, and Velázquez.

HIGHLIGHTS

- *Adoration of St. Vincent*, Nuno Gonçalves
- Cook Triptych, Grão Vasco
- *Annunciation*, Frei Carlos
- *Temptation of St. Antony*, Hieronymus Bosch
- *Madonna and Child*, Memling
- *St. Jerome*, Albrecht Dürer
- *St. Augustine*, Piero della Francesca
- French silver tableware
- Japanese Namban screens

INFORMATION

- ✚ G9
- ✉ Rua das Janelas Verdes- Jardim 9 de Abril
- ☎ 213 912 800
- ◷ Wed–Sun 10–6; Tue 2–6
- 🍴 Small bar and restaurant
- 🚌 7, 40, 49, 51, 60; tram 15, 18
- 🚉 Santos (Cascais line)
- ♿ Good: elevator, small steps
- 💲 Moderate
- ↔ Basílica da Estrela (➤ 32)

Top: the Adoration of St. Vincent. Left: statue of St. Trinity

BASÍLICA DA ESTRELA

HIGHLIGHTS

- Façade
- Twin towers
- Tomb of Dona Maria I
- Views from the dome
- Jardim da Estrela

INFORMATION

- G8
- Praça da Estrela
- 213 960 915
- Daily 8–12:30, 3–7:30
- Rato
- 20, 22, 38; tram 25, 28
- Poor
- Free
- Museu Nacional de Arte Antiga (▶ 31)

A massive dome crowns the Basílica (interior, top)

The chill austerity of neo-classical architecture is not to everyone's liking, but it is difficult to remain unaffected by the sheer scale of a building like the Estrela basilica —not to mention the sweeping views from its dome.

Offering Like the Palácio de Fronteira, the Basílica da Estrela lies some way from the city center—about a mile to the west of the Bairro Alto—but it is more than worth the effort required to see it. You will be doubly rewarded if you combine a trip here with a visit to the Jardim de Estrela (Jardim Guerra Junqueiro), one of the city's most beautiful gardens (▶ 56). The basilica, a monumental white edifice, was founded by Dona Maria I in 1779 as a votive offering for the birth of a son. Begun in the same year, it is a neo-classical masterpiece, and one of Lisbon's most imposing 18th-century buildings.

Impressive The church's architects, Mateus Vicente and Reinaldo Manuel, were influenced by the convent at Mafra (▶ 21), a building whose main attribute is size. Size is also the basilica's defining feature, the austere interior a cavernous expanse of chill marble. To the left of the high altar lies the tomb of Dona Maria I, who died in Brazil in 1816 and whose body was returned to Portugal for burial six years later. Unlike male scions of the Bragança royal dynasty, who were embalmed for posterity, Maria was simply adorned with herbs and enclosed in three tight-closing coffins, one inside the other. It is said that when these were opened to transfer the body back to Portugal, two ladies-in-waiting assisting in the ceremony fainted at the stench from the putrefied corpse.

10 ✓

MUSEU CALOUSTE GULBENKIAN

If you were given the job of putting together an art gallery with unlimited funds, you would come up with something pretty close to the Gulbenkian. Its range is complete, from ancient to modern, famous to obscure, and from east to west.

Bequest to the nation The Gulbenkian is Portugal's single greatest museum. Run by the Fundação Calouste Gulbenkian, it is one of the countless artistic and cultural initiatives financed by a bequest from Calouste Gulbenkian (1869–1955), an Armenian oil magnate. It was built between 1964 and 1969 by the architects Alberto Passoal, Pedro Cid, and Ruy Athouguia on a 17-acre site. Calouste Gulbenkian's private art collection makes up the bulk of the museum's collection, which is divided into two sections: the first deals with ancient and Oriental exhibits, the second with European art and artifacts.

Stunning collection The European section embraces paintings, sculptures, and the decorative arts. Exhibits are arranged chronologically and, wherever possible, according to school and nationality. The paintings include works by Manet, Degas, Renoir, Van Dyck, Frans Hals, Ghirlandaio, Turner, and Gainsborough. Pride of place goes to Rembrandt's *Alexander the Great* and captivating *Portrait of an Old Man*. Among the wealth of tapestries, furniture, silverware, and other beautiful artifacts, look out in particular for the stunning jewelry by René Lalique (in a reverentially darkened room at the end of the gallery). In the ancient and Oriental sections, the highlights include Chinese porcelain, Japanese lacquer work, and silk and wool carpets. End your visit with a walk in the foundation's lovely gardens. There is also a tasteful café in the museum basement.

HIGHLIGHTS

- Rembrandt paintings
- Islamic ceramics
- Lalique jewelry and glass
- Carpets
- French ivory diptychs

Rembrandt's Portrait of an Old Man *Top: Famille Rose porcelain*

INFORMATION

- ✚ G5
- ✉ Avenida de Berna 45
- ☎ 217 823 000
- 🕐 Tue 12–6; Wed–Sun 10–6. Closed public hols
- 🍴 Café
- Ⓜ São Sebastião/Praça de Espanha
- 🚌 16, 26, 31, 46, 56
- 🚕 Rego
- ♿ Excellent
- 🎟 Moderate. Free on Sun
- ↔ Centro de Arte Moderna (► 34)
- ❓ Downhill from Metro, turn right after 300 yards

CENTRO DE ARTE MODERNA

HIGHLIGHTS

- Henry Moore
- Amadeu de Souza-Cardoso
- Guilherme Santa Rita
- Paula Rego
- João Cutileiro
- Vieira da Silva
- Julio Pomar
- Costa Pinheiro

INFORMATION

✚ G5

✉ Rua Dr. Nicolau de Bettencourt

☎ 217 823 483/212 782 3474

🕐 Tue 2–6; Wed–Sun 10–6. Closed public hols. Occasional late opening in summer

Ⓜ São Sebastião/Praça de Espanha

🚌 16, 26, 31, 46, 56

🚉 Rego

♿ Good

Ⓘ Moderate. Free on Sun

↔ Museu Calouste Gulbenkian (➤ 33)

Top: Time, P. Rego.
Below: painting by A. de Souza-Cardoso

The names of modern Portuguese artists will be unfamiliar to most people, but there's no better place to become acquainted with their work than this superlative state-of-the-art gallery sponsored by the Calouste Gulbenkian Foundation.

Parkland gem Lisbon's Center for Modern Art lies just around the corner from the better-known Museu Calouste Gulbenkian. Like its near neighbor, it was made possible by the legacy of Calouste Gulbenkian, the Armenian oil magnate, who left his art collection and a slice of his fortune to Portugal. The center is set in the same park, and is housed in a beautiful modern building designed by the British architect Sir Leslie Martin and opened in 1983. The museum's airy exhibition space—all clean lines and abundant greenery—is a pleasure in itself, admirably complementing a collection of over 10,000 works of art.

National collection The parkland surrounding the museum is scattered with sculptures, of which the most notable is the *Reclining Woman* by Henry Moore, close to the main entrance. Inside, the gallery's eminent Portuguese painters include Amadeu de Souza-Cardoso and Guilherme Santa Rita, both of whom were influenced by the Italian Futurists. In acknowledging the work of foreign painters, the pair were typical of Portuguese artists, most of whom worked or studied abroad. By following such foreign styles and not establishing their own movement few artists from Portugal are said to to have strongly influenced the evolution of modern art. Almada Negreiros is credited as founder of Portuguese modernism, and others who have become known outside Portugal include Paula Rego, João Cutileiro, Vieira da Silva, Julio Pomar, and Costa Pinheiro.

12

BAIRRO ALTO

Traditionally the bohemian haunt of students, artists, and writers, the narrow cobbled streets of the Bairro Alto, packed with cafés, restaurants, bars, and the home of the traditional fado singing, are an essential feature of any visit to the city.

Nightlife The Bairro Alto, or Upper Town, is one of Lisbon's liveliest and most distinctive quarters, and one of the five loosely defined neighborhoods that make up the heart of the old city. Traditionally a working-class area, it was hardly damaged by the 1755 earthquake, and rises in a close-knit grid of 16th-century streets up the steep slopes west of the Chiado and Baixa districts. During the day, its quiet corners are filled with the sort of evocative scenes you find all over Lisbon—washing strung from the windows and ragamuffin children playing in the streets. As night falls, by contrast, the restaurants and bars open and by 10PM the strains of fado (➤ 82) can be heard as the area becomes the principal focus of Lisbon's nightlife.

Sights Exploring the Bairro's streets is an activity worth pursuing for its own sake, but some sights deserve special attention. These include the Elevador de Santa Justa, a clanking old elevator built in 1902, and the Elevador da Glória, a funicular built in 1885. Both save you a lot of climbing by carrying you up from the Baixa district below. Other sights are the Solar do Vinho do Porto, run by the Port Wine Institute (see panel, ➤ 78) and the Igreja de São Roque (➤ 36). The Miradouro de São Pedro de Alcântara has some fine views over the city (➤ 53).

HIGHLIGHTS

- Elevador de Santa Justa
- Elevador da Glória
- Solar do Vinho do Porto
- Igreja de São Roque
- Miradouro de São Pedro de Alcântara (➤ 53)
- Rua de Atalaia (shopping)
- Rua do Diário de Notícias (shopping)

INFORMATION

Left: the Elevador de Santa Justa takes you up to Chiado and the Bairro Alto beyond (top)

13

IGREJA DE SÃO ROQUE

HIGHLIGHTS

- Painted wooden ceiling
- Capela de São Roque
- Tile decoration
- Capela de São João Baptista
- Mosaics

INFORMATION

- ✚ H8; all
- ✉ Largo Trindade Coelho
- ☎ 213 235 381
- 🕐 Museum: Tue–Sun 10–5. Closed public hols. Church daily 8:30–6
- 🚇 Baixa-Chiado
- 🚌 58, 100
- ♿ Poor
- 🎫 Church free. Museum inexpensive; free on Sun and public hols
- ↔ Bairro Alto (➤ 35), Chiado (➤ 37), Museu Arqueológico do Carmo (➤ 38)

Asked to highlight the most extravagant piece of decorative folly in Lisbon, you would have no hesitation in plumping for the Igreja de São Roque, and in particular its chapels, which groan under the weight of gold, gilt, marble, and other precious materials.

Lavish interior Little in the plain façade of this church prepares you for the decorative splendor within. Commissioned by the Jesuits in the 16th century, the building of 1565 was the work of Filippo Terzi, also responsible for the church of São Vicente across the city. His original façade fell victim to the 1755 earthquake, but not the interior, which was saved, according to popular belief, by the personal intervention of St. Roch (São Roque). Inside, the trompe l'œil painting on the ceiling is a triumph, while each of the eight chapels lining the nave is a decorative masterpiece. The third on the right, the Capela de São Roque, features some of the finest *azulejos* (tiles) in the city, the work of Francisco de Matos in 1584, his only known commission.

Chapel The fourth chapel on the left, the Capela de São João Baptista, though less immediately impressive, has been called the most expensive chapel for its size ever built. Commissioned in 1742 by João V, it was designed by Vanvitelli, the papal architect, and built in Rome. There it was blessed by Pope Benedict XIV before being shipped to Lisbon, where its ensemble of precious materials— ivory, amethyst, porphyry, and Carrara marble among others—was reassembled. Note the chapel's "paintings," which are not paintings but extraordinarily detailed mosaics. Beside the church is the Museu de Arte Sacra, with a rich collection of paintings, embroidery, and ecclesiastical plate.

Baroque extravagance in São Roque's Capela de Nossa Sra da Assumpa

CHIADO

Despite its partial destruction by fire in 1988, today the Chiado thrives. Modern boutiques and department stores, hidden behind beautifully restored facades, sit harmoniously beside Lisbon's oldest stores and stylish wood-paneled cafés.

District The Chiado is one of the five loosely defined districts that make up the heart of old Lisbon. Named after the poet António Ribeiro who was nicknamed O Chiado, meaning "Squeaky," it lies just alongside the Baixa, spreading across the first of the slopes that rise westwards to the Bairro Alto. Known primarily as a shopping district, it embraces not only the main Largo do Chiado, but also a range of streets centered on Rua Garrett and Rua do Carmo. Affluent and fashionable, its streets contain many luxury stores and fine old cafés, notably A Brasileira in Rua Garrett. Also here are the Teatro São Carlos opera house and the Igreja dos Mártires, the latter built over the site of a Crusader burial ground and encampment.

Destruction On August 25, 1988, the Chiado achieved unwanted fame when it was ravaged by fire. The conflagration is thought to have started in a store on Rua do Carmo, and devastated four blocks of the district before being brought under control. Some 2,000 people lost their jobs, and many old buildings were gutted, including the famous Ferrari coffee-house and Grandella department store. In the disaster's aftermath, the Mayor of Lisbon entrusted the reconstruction of the area to Alvaro Siza Vieira, a celebrated Portuguese architect, who resolved to rebuild the district to a classical plan in keeping with the existing structures. Much of the rebuilding and restoration has now been successfully completed.

HIGHLIGHTS

- Rua Garrett
- Teatro de São Carlos
- Igreja dos Mártires
- Museu Arqueológico do Carmo (➤ 38)
- Café A Brasileira (➤ 69)
- Museu do Chiado (➤ 51)

INFORMATION

- ✛ H8; alll
- ✉ São Carlos-Largo de São Carlos
- 🍴 Cafés, bars, and restaurants
- Ⓜ Baixa-Chiado
- 🚌 58,100; tram 15, 18, 28
- ♿ Poor
- ↔ Igreja de São Roque (➤ 36), Rossio (➤ 39), Bairro Alto (➤ 35)

15

MUSEU ARQUEOLÓGICO DO CARMO

HIGHLIGHTS

- Church ruins
- Shrunken heads
- Mummies
- Gothic tombs
- Bronze Age pottery
- Tiles
- Prehistoric artifacts

INFORMATION

- H8; alII
- Convento do Carmo, Largo do Carmo
- 213 460 473
- Apr–Sep: Tue–Sun 10–6. Oct–Mar: Tue–Sun 10–1. Closed public hols
- Baixa-Chiado
- 58, 100; tram 28. Elevador de Santa Justa
- Poor
- Inexpensive
- Chiado (➤ 37), Rossio (➤ 39), Baixa (➤ 40), Igreja de São Roque (➤ 36)
- At time of writing, museum still closed for repair owing to structural damage. Due to open early 2001

While modern, well-organized museums such as the Gulbenkian are a joy, you can still find something very appealing about the wonderfully jumbled and eccentric collection of exhibits in the Museu Arqueológico do Carmo.

Location The archeological museum is within the ruins of the Convento do Carmo, a Carmelite convent built by Nun' Álvares Pereira. He was a general and companion-in-arms to João I at the Battle of Aljubarrota in 1385, which secured Portuguese independence from Castile for two hundred years. Until 1755, when the convent church was toppled by the Great Earthquake, it was the largest church in the city. Over the years, its ruins were used as a graveyard, municipal dump, and military stable. Today its soaring Gothic interior is largely open to the Lisbon sky, the nave and chancel now a threadbare garden full of cats, flowers, and shattered statuary before becoming a museum.

Eccentric The museum's exhibits are a slightly disorganized and eccentric mixture, though none the worse for that, their eclectic jumble constituting part of their appeal. They include two large tombs, one belonging to Ferdinand I, King of Portugal from 1367 to 1382, the other to Gonçalo de Souza, chancellor to Henry the Navigator. The stone bust in the chancel is thought to be the oldest known image of Afonso Henriques, Portugal's first king. Older exhibits include prehistoric and Visigothic artifacts, notably flints, arrowheads, and pottery, together with Roman remains and a large number of Hebrew, Arabic, and other stone inscriptions. The more eccentric displays include shrunken heads, two South American mummies, and many tiles and florid pieces of sculpture.

Metallurgy tools from Vila Nova de São Pedro hillfort, c3000 bc

ROSSIO

Every city has its main square, and Lisbon's is the Rossio, though it is not the prettiest place to take a break from sightseeing. There is little greenery and a lot of traffic, but there is no doubting its appeal as a natural meeting place for visitors and locals alike.

Turbulent past The Rossio, also known as Praça Dom Pedro IV, is Lisbon's natural focus, a large and bustling square close to one of the city's main stations, the Chiado shopping district, and the Baixa. It dates from around the 13th century, though its present appearance is due mostly to the Marquês de Pombal (▶ 12), and 19th-century rebuilding. Between 1534 and 1820, the Inquisitors' palace stood on the north side, and in the 16th century the Inquisitors' victims —convicted heretics—were burned in the square. The Inquisition's sentences were handed down from São Domingos, a church to the east, still closed after a fire in the 1950s.

Relaxing present Today the square is lined with cafés and stores, some of which have fine turn-of-the-century facades. Many of the cafés have outside tables, favored vantage points from which to watch the world go by. Two of the most popular cafés are Nicola (▶ 69) on the western flank of the square and Suiça (▶ 69) on the eastern. The statue (1870) at the heart of the square is Dom Pedro IV, though it was sculpted as Maximilian of Mexico. It was passing through Lisbon on the way to Mexico, and remained when news broke of Maximilian's assassination. The square's grandest building, the Teatro Nacional de Dona Maria, was built in the 1840s over the site of the former Inquisitors' palace.

DID YOU KNOW?

- The Rossio is the most expensive property on the Portuguese "Monopoly" board

HIGHLIGHTS

- Cafés (▶ 69)
- Shop fronts
- Statue of Dom Pedro IV
- Fountain
- Teatro Nacional
- Facade of Estação do Rossio (station)

INFORMATION

- ✛ H8–J8; bIII
- ✉ Praça Dom Pedro IV
- 🍴 Cafés, bars, and restaurants
- 🚇 Rossio
- 🚌 All services to the Rossio
- ♿ Poor
- ↔ Baixa (▶ 40), Museu Arqueológico do Carmo (▶ 38), Chiado (▶ 37), Praça do Comércio (▶ 41)

Top: Rossio railroad station's fine facade. Left: Statue of Dom Pedro IV

17

BAIXA

HIGHLIGHTS

- Art deco store fronts
- Mosaic pavements
- Cobbled streets

INFORMATION

- J8; bIII
- Streets between the Rossio and Praça do Comércio
- Cafés, bars, and restaurants
- Rossio/Baixa-Chiado
- All services to the Rossio and Praça do Comércio
- Poor
- Praça do Comércio (➤ 41), Rossio (➤ 39), Sé (➤ 42), Castelo de São Jorge (➤ 43), Alfama (➤ 44)

The tiny Baixa district, lodged between the hills of the Chiado and Alfama, with its planned network of 18th-century cobbled streets, its many elaborate store fronts and lively commercial bustle, forms the heart of old Lisbon.

Pombal's vision A grid of ordered streets, the Baixa district stretches from the Rossio in the north to the Praça do Comércio in the south, with the Chiado rising to the west and the Alfama to the east. Once this low-lying area was probably centered on a stream, with houses built on stilts to escape flooding. Its appearance was changed beyond all recognition following the 1755 earthquake, when the Marquês de Pombal decided to rebuild the area along strictly rational lines (➤ 12). The forthright First Minister decreed that all new streets should be "40 feet in width, with pavements on either side protected from wheeled traffic by stone pillars, as in London."

Tradition Pombal's dream was realized with the help of a military engineer, Eugénio dos Santos, and the result has been described by some as one of the finest European architectural achievements of the age. To others the district's relentless simplicity and symmetry made it appear soulless. Today there is no denying the streets' lively old-fashioned charm, nor the appeal of the mosaic-patterned pavements, tiled facades, and lovely old store fronts. The pedestrian-only Rua Augusta is the area's main axis. Many minor streets bear names relating to the trades once practised there—Rua da Prata (silversmiths), Rua Áurea (formerly Rua do Ouro—goldsmiths), and Rua dos Sapateiros (cobblers).

Restoration is reviving the Baixa's charm

PRAÇA DO COMÉRCIO

The Praça do Comércio, the centerpiece of the Marquês de Pombal's reconstruction of 1758, is dominated by the imposing statue of José I. It provides a triumphal entrance to the city from the airy open spaces of the waterfront.

Gateway Locally the square is known as the Terreiro do Paço, or Terrace of the Palace, an allusion to the 16th-century Royal Palace that stood here until it was almost completely destroyed by the 1755 earthquake. At its heart stands an equestrian statue of José I, king at the time of the 1755 earthquake, the blackened luster of its bronze giving rise to the Praça's nickname "Black Horse Square." It took some 1,000 people almost four days to move the statue into position. The palace's old steps still climb up from the waterfront, but today the square is dominated by the vast, 19th-century triumphal arch on its northern flank, and by ranks of imposing arcades and neo-classical government offices. In 1908, King Carlos I was assassinated together with Luis Filipe, his son and heir, in the corner of the square near Rua do Arsenal.

Revival Now that the city authorities have banned its use as a parking lot, the Praca do Comércio is once again one of Lisbon's most majestic squares. Its grand spaces and imposing buildings, once compromised, have been released from the motorcar's tyranny and the square can again reveal its intended effect—to serve as a dramatic gateway from the sea, and as an antechamber to the well-ordered streets of the Baixa and the rest of the city.

HIGHLIGHTS

- View from the waterfront
- Triumphal arch
- Arcades
- Statue of Dom José I

INFORMATION

- ➕ J8; bIV
- ✉ Praça do Comércio
- 🚇 Rossio
- 🚌 All services to Praça do Comércio
- ♿ Good
- 🎟 Free
- ↔ Baixa (➤ 40), Sé (➤ 42), Rossio (➤ 39), Castelo de São Jorge (➤ 43)

José I surveys the Praça do Comércio

19

SÉ

HIGHLIGHTS

- Twin towers
- Rose window
- Baptismal font
- Bartolomeu Chapel (1324)
- Nativity, Joaquim Machado de Castro (1766)
- Tomb of Lopo Fernandes Pacheco
- Cloisters
- Treasury
- Reliquary of St. Vincent
- Dom José I monstrance

INFORMATION

- ✚ J8; cIII
- ✉ Largo da Sé
- ☎ 218 873 258
- 🕐 Museum and cathedral: Mon–Sat 10–5
- 🚇 Rossio/Baixa-Chiado
- 🚌 28, 37; tram 12, 28
- ♿ Poor
- 💰 Cathedral: free Cloister: inexpensive, free on Sun
- ↔ Praça do Comércio (➤ 41), Baixa (➤ 40), Castelo de São Jorge (➤ 43)
- ❓ The cloister is reached from the high altar end, on the left

Nothing evokes a stronger sense of Lisbon's long history than views of the formidable cathedral, whose ancient stone towers can be seen above the rooftops from the Baixa and the viewpoints of the Bairro Alto.

History Lisbon's cathedral was begun around 1150, soon after Afonso Henriques, Portugal's first king, had captured the city from the Moors. It was the city's first church, and legend claims it stands on the site of a mosque. Like other Portuguese cathedrals of similar vintage—Évora, Porto, Coimbra—it has a fortress-like appearance, the result of its plain Romanesque design

and the tumultuous times in which it was built, when there was still a threat from the Moors. Much of its original shell survives, notably its distinctive squat towers, which unlike the old chancel withstood the earthquakes of 1344 and 1755, as well as the attentions of restorers.

Interior On the left as you enter the church is a font, reputedly used in 1195 to baptize St. Antony of Padua, who was born in Lisbon. The first chapel on the left features an intricately carved Nativity scene, the work of 18th-century sculptor Joaquim Machado de Castro. More beautiful still is the tomb of Lopo Fernandes Pacheco, a courtier of Afonso IV, in the chapel on the right of the gothic ambulatory. The ruined 13th-century Gothic cloister is worth seeing for its lovely sculptural fragments.

Top: the tomb of Pacheco. Above: the massive Romanesque front of the Sé

20

CASTELO DE SÃO JORGE

Every city needs at least one place like Lisbon's ancient fortress. With its breath-taking views and lovely gardens, it provides a shady oasis where you can retreat from the rigors of sightseeing to enjoy an hour or two's peace and quiet.

Defense Lisbon's evocatively situated castle marks the city's birthplace, the spot where Phoenician traders probably first made camp, attracted by the area's fine natural harbor, its easily defended position, and the agricultural potential of its fertile hinterland. Later it was fortified by the Romans, Visigoths, and Moors, the defeat of the last, at the hands of Afonso Henriques in 1147, marking a turning point in the campaign to oust the Moors from Portugal. Henriques took the fortress after a 17-week siege, a victory tainted by the behavior of his British and French allies—supposedly Christian Crusaders—who ran amok, pillaging and murdering Moors and Christians alike.

Views Today the castle's walls have been rather over-restored. Its pristine stonework makes it hard to believe that much of the 12th-century original remains, though its lofty site and beautiful grounds are irresistible. The outer walls enclose the little district of Santa Cruz, one of the medieval jewels of the old Alfama district. A statue of Afonso Henriques glowers over the main entrance, beyond which lies a lovely array of verdant terraces and leafy walkways. Ducks and swans glide across limpid pools, while other birds, some exotic, flit across the manicured lawns. This is a delightful place to relax or stroll for an hour or so, with picnic tables on hand. Best of all, however, are the superlative views over the rooftops from the old Moorish battlements, which rise over 80 feet above the Alfama.

DID YOU KNOW?

- Portugal's early kings occupied the Alcáçova, the castle's former Moorish palace
- The castle's name, São Jorge (St. George), reputedly commemorates the Anglo-Portuguese pact of 1371
- The Portuguese call the castle belvedere the "ancient window," because of its views

HIGHLIGHTS

- Views
- Gardens
- Battlemented walls
- Ten towers
- Parade ground

INFORMATION

- ✚ J8; cIII
- ✉ Rua Costa do Castelo
- 🕐 Apr–Sep: daily 9–9. Oct–Mar: daily 9–7
- 🚌 37; tram 28, 12
- ♿ Poor
- 🎫 Free
- ↔ Alfama (➤ 44), Museu das Artes Decorativas (➤ 45), Baixa (➤ 40), Rossio (➤ 39), Sé (➤ 42), Campo de Santa Clara (➤ 46)

ALFAMA

This warren of atmospheric old streets is tailor-made for random exploration. Its alleys, often no more than 1 yard wide, hanging washing, flower-laden windows, and beautifully preserved tile-fronted mansions create a step back in time.

Springs Of all Lisbon's old quarters, none is more evocative or pleasant to explore than the Alfama, a labyrinth of timeless vignettes and Medina-like streets that still have an Arabic feel. The area takes its name from a Moorish word, *alhama*, or fountain, a reference to the hot springs in Largo das Alcaçárias. As a distinct enclave, however, it is much older, probably dating back to the first Phoenician or Roman traders who settled the site of the present-day Castelo. Between 711 and 1147, it became an important Moorish suburb, and later still the home of the city's first churches. In time, it became a retreat for the city's élite, losing its cachet only after the 1755 earthquake.

Top: walks depicted in tiles. Above: street scene

Sights Today for the most part the area is a robust and old-fashioned residential neighborhood, though the restorers, gentrifying many of the once humble dwellings, the restaurants and the first trendy stores are beginning to take the edge off its pristine appeal. The best way to see the district is to wander at random amid the streets and half-hidden squares—maps are almost useless here. Streets you might try to head for include the Rua de São Pedro, Rua São Miguel, Beco de Cardosa, the Pátio das Flores, Largo de São Rafael, and Rua dos Remédios. Try also to take in the viewpoints at Largo das Portas do Sol and the Miradouro de Santa Luzia (which has several good cafés).

MUSEU DAS ARTES DECORATIVAS

This beautifully restored 17th-century palace houses a stunning collection of furniture, carpets, and antiques displayed in a wonderful period setting, giving the visitor a picture of upper-class Lisbon life in the 18th and 19th centuries.

Bequest Lisbon's beguiling Museum of the Decorative Arts is housed in the 17th-century palace of the Counts of Azurara, former home of Ricardo do Espírito Santo Silva (1900–1955) a Portuguese philanthropist. He left the house and his private collection of art and artifacts to the nation in 1953. Both house and collection, run by the Espírito Santo Silva Foundation, are now open to the public. The foundation also supports a series of workshops (next door to the museum) in which you can watch people involved in such traditional skills as bookbinding, gilding, wood-carving, and cabinet-making.

Exquisite home Santo Silva had exceptional taste, with the result that his collection embraces some of the finest examples of Portuguese and other art and artifacts. The palace itself is beautiful with its original 17th-century wooden floors, painted ceilings, and panels of blue and white *azulejos* (tiles) an ideal setting for the exceptional furniture, antiques, tapestries, and rugs from Arraiolos, a central Portugeuse town renowned for its exquisite carpets. Also on display are porcelain and silverware, together with various *objets d'art* of both Portuguese and Indo-Portuguese origin. Perhaps the most captivating areas of the museum to visit are the bedrooms, complete with tiny four-poster beds, and the upstairs dining room, with its ancient grandfather clock and beautiful painted ceiling.

HIGHLIGHTS

- Palace
- Furniture
- Carpets
- Painted ceilings
- Bedrooms
- Tapestries
- Silverware
- Inlaid chess table

INFORMATION

- ✚ J8; cIII
- ✉ Largo das Portas do Sol 2
- ☎ 218 884 600
- ◷ Wed–Mon 10–5. Closed public hols
- 🍴 Café
- Ⓠ Rossio
- 🚌 37; tram 12, 28
- ♿ Very poor: many stairs
- 💰 Expensive
- ↔ Alfama (► 44), Campo de Santa Clara (► 46), Castelo de São Jorge (► 43)

Above: the palace is a superb setting. Top: Portuguese silverware

23

CAMPO DE SANTA CLARA

HIGHLIGHTS

- Feira da Ladra
- Santa Engrácia
- São Vicente de Fora
- Jardim Boto Machado
- Miradouro da Senhora do Monte
- Museu Nacional Militar

INFORMATION

- K7
- Campo de Santa Clara
- Feira da Ladra: Tue 7AM–1PM; Sat 7AM–4PM
- Cafés
- 12, 37, 104, 105, 107 and then walk; tram 28 direct
- Poor
- Museu das Artes Decorativas (➤ 45), Alfama (➤ 44)
- Watch for pickpockets

Campo de Santa Clara deserves a special mention for its churches, but should preferably be visited on one of its market days when regular stalls are set up alongside individuals selling anything from shoe insoles to used car batteries.

Colorful market Campo de Santa Clara lies on the eastern margins of the Alfama district, one of Lisbon's most atmospheric quarters. The square and its surrounding streets are best known for their flea market, the Feira da Ladra (the "Thieves' Market"), which takes place here on Tuesday morning and all day Saturday. The Feira's covered stalls (at the center of the square) sell a predictable assortment of market goods—food, shoes, inexpensive clothes, and household items—while the peripheral stalls deal in books, old postcards, and miscellaneous bric-a-brac. Don't be fooled; any genuine bargains are few, but you can spend an enjoyable morning browsing here.

Vistas Market or no, the area around Campo de Santa Clara would still be worth exploring. Two of the city's more interesting churches are near by: Santa Engrácia (➤ 54) to the southeast and São Vicente de Fora (➤ 55) to the northwest, the former completed only in 1966, the latter of 1704, the burial place of many of Portugal's kings and queens. At the heart of the square itself is the Jardim Boto Machado, a small garden full of palms and exotic plants, with a fine view over the city to the south. To the north are the Palácio Lavradio, home to the military tribunal, and another excellent viewpoint, the Miradouro da Senhora do Monte. A short walk to the south of the square lies the Museu Nacional Militar, the military museum, in the 18th-century former arsenal (➤ 52).

The popular flea market held in the Campo de Santa Clara

IGREJA DA MADRE DE DEUS

Although not close to the center, this church has some of the city's most opulent decoration. Its lavish gilt baroque pulpit and altar, walls covered with tiles and 16th–17th century paintings, make it an enticing double bill when seen with the adjoining Museu Nacional do Azulejo.

Convent Like Belém to the west, this grand and sumptuously decorated church, some 2 miles east of the Baixa, is one of the few sights in Lisbon worth leaving the city center to see. Originally part of a larger convent, it was founded in 1509 by Dona Leonor, widow of Dom João II. Later it was expanded by João III, only to be virtually destroyed during the 1755 earthquake. Subsequent rebuilding turned the church's interior into one of the most magnificent in the city, but the exterior's Manueline doorway and the crypt (with a grandiose altar and 16th-century Seville tiles) have survived from Leonor's earlier foundation.

Elaborate church The interior is a masterpiece of decorative excess, laden with gilded wood and tiles and decorated with several glorious paintings. Scenes from the Life of the Virgin fill the coffered main vault, paintings high on the walls depict scenes from the Life of St. Francis (right wall when facing the altar) and the Life of St. Clare (left wall when facing altar). The lower walls are covered in beautiful blue and white 18th-century Dutch tiles. In the even more breathtaking chapter house, virtually every surface is adorned with tiles or gilt-framed paintings. Make a point of seeing also the Capela de Santo António and the sacristy, which are similarly embellished.

HIGHLIGHTS

- Manueline doorway
- Gilded woodwork
- Vault paintings
- Wall paintings
- Chapter house
- Sacristy
- Capela de Santo António
- Crypt

INFORMATION

- ✚ L6
- ✉ Rua da Madre de Deus 4
- ☎ 218 147 747
- ◷ Wed–Sun 10–6; Tue 2–6
- ▣ 18, 42, 59, 104, 105
- ♿ Poor
- 🎟 Free
- ↔ Museu Nacional do Azulejo
  (► 48)

The main altar in its gilded glory

25

MUSEU NACIONAL DO AZULEJO

HIGHLIGHTS

- Tiled Manueline cloisters
- Café
- Lisbon cityscape (1738)
- Tiled Nativity (1580)
- Food tiles
- Modern Metro tiles
- Tiled battle scenes

INFORMATION

- L6
- Rua da Madre de Deus 4
- 218 847 747
- Wed–Sun 10–6; Tue 2–6
- Café
- 18, 42, 59, 104, 105
- Poor
- Moderate. Free on Sun and public hols until 2
- Igreja da Madre de Deus (➤ 47)

Situated some 2 miles from the city center, this lovely museum, housed in tranquil monastic cloisters, traces the history of tile-making. Through Moorish, Hispanic, and Dutch influences, here you'll see the Portuguese emerge as masters of their craft.

Simple and sophisticated The museum's earliest *azulejos* (a corruption of the Arabic word *azraq* (azure) or *zalayja*, meaning a smooth stone or polished terra-cotta) date from the beginning of the 16th century. Later exhibits show how simple, single-color designs gave way to the more sophisticated patterning allowed by the new majolica techniques imported from Italy. As the art developed, *azulejos* became still more complex and colorful. Later still, they were influenced by the single-motif patterns of Dutch tiles and by the fashion for blue and white inspired by the arrival of Ming dynasty porcelain in Europe. Simpler designs also resulted from the 1755 earthquake, when large numbers of cheap decorative tiles were required for rebuilding.

Museum high points Among the museum's many highlights look out in particular for the 105-foot tiled cityscape of Lisbon, made in 1738 prior to the 1755 earthquake, and the small Manueline cloister decorated with its original 16th- and 17th-century tiles. Also, don't miss the fine, 1580 polychrome tile picture of Nossa Senhora da Vida, a nativity scene. There are delightful 18th-century blue-and-white tile scenes of every day life such as a doctor giving an injection. Further displays depict battle scenes, and there is a collection of modern Metro tiles by well-known artists such as Julio Pomar and Viera da Silva. The museum restaurant is decorated with mouthwatering food *azulejos* of hams, rabbits, and other delicacies.

The 18th-century tiled cityscape of Lisbon

LISBON's
best

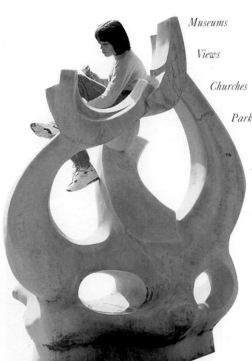

49

MUSEUMS

Twentieth century design

As well as home to temporary exhibitions and performing arts, the immense but outstanding Centro Cultural de Belém now houses the Museo do Design. The collection is divided into three sections entitled Luxury, Pop, and Cool, and illustrates the forms, concepts, and function of objects from the 20th century.

⊞ B10 ⊠ Praça do Império ☎ 213 612 934 ④ Daily 11–5 🚍 27, 28, 29, 43, 49, 51; tram 15 🚊 Belém (Cascais line) from Cais do Sodré 🎟 Moderate

MUSEU NACIONAL DE ARTE POPULAR

Lisbon's National Folk Art Museum is near the waterfront in Belém. It was established in 1948 and its typical postwar utilitarian architecture makes it a bit dated, but there are enough interesting exhibits to merit a quick visit. It looks at Portugal's folk art and traditions province by province, with five rooms of clothes, paintings, rugs, votive offerings, musical instruments, agricultural implements, pottery, wickerwork, and other craft items. The exhibits are complemented by photographs and striking wall paintings, the latter the work of leading modern Portuguese artists such as Paulo Ferreira, Carlos Botelho, and Tomás de Melo.

⊞ B10 ⊠ Avenida de Brasília ☎ 213 011 282 ④ Tue–Sun 10–12:30, 2–5 🚍 27, 28, 43, 49, 51; tram 15 🎟 Inexpensive. Free Sun morning ❓ Access from Mosteiro dos Jerónimos is via the waterfront and a passage under the road and railroad

Exhibits in the Museu de Arte Popular are backed by photographs and paintings

MUSEU DA CIÊNCIA

Permanent hands-on science exhibits along with temporary thematic exhibitions all help to make science more accessible. Check out the antique scientific instrument display.

🕂 G/H7 ✉ Rua da Escola Politécnica 56 ☎ 213 961 521/22/23 🕙 Mon–Sun 10–1, 2–5 🚌 58 💲 Inexpensive. Free on Sat

MUSEU DO CHIADO

Housed in a 13th-century abbey, this museum is devoted to Portuguese painting and sculpture. It was refurbished in 1994 with dramatic high brick vaults and polished gray marble, by the French architect Jean-Michel Wilmotte. Concentrating on the years 1850–1950, it delves into realism, romanticism, symbolism, and modernism. Worth seeing are *A Sesta* by Almada Negreiros; the *Concerto de Amadores* by Columbano; and Soares dos Reis's *O Desterrado*.

🕂 H8 ✉ Rua Serpa Pinto 6 ☎ 213 432 148/9 🕙 Wed–Sun 10–6; Tue 2–6 🍴 Café 🚌 58, 100; tram 15, 28 💲 Inexpensive. Free Sun and public hols until 2

A Sesta, *Almada Negreiros (1939)*

MUSEU DA CIDADE

The Museum of the City lies north of the city center in the northwest corner of the Campo Grande. A stimulating museum in a lovely setting, it uses paintings, prints, and drawings to trace the development of Lisbon across the centuries. Highlights include a model of pre-earthquake Lisbon, a 17th-century painting showing the Praça do Comércio before the Marqués de Pombal remodeled it, and a picture of the poet Fernando Pessoa, painted in 1954, 19 years after his death.

🕂 G3 ✉ Campo Grande 245 ☎ 217 591 617 🕙 Tue–Sun 10–1, 2–6 🚇 Campo Grande 🚌 1, 3, 7, 33, 36, 47, 50, 68, 85, 101, 102, 108 💲 Inexpensive. Free on Sun

MUSEU ETNOLÓGICO DA SOCIEDADE DE GEOGRAFIA

This little gem in the city center displays objects from Portugal's former colonies in Africa and Asia, in a remarkable late 19th-century room. Opening times are limited.

🕂 H7; all ✉ Rua das Portas de Santo Antão 100 ☎ 213 425 401 🕙 Mon, Wed, Fri 11–1, 3–5 🚇 Restauradores 🚌 1, 2, 9, 21, 44, 45 💲 Inexpensive

MUSEU DA MARIONETA

This fascinating museum displays indigenous puppets from Japan, Thailand, Burma, and Indonesia, some over 3 feet in height. There are also occasional puppet shows. Try not to be put off by the shabby square and very down-at-heel building in which the museum is housed, close to the Castelo's eastern entrance.

🕂 J8; cIII ✉ Largo Rodrigues de Freitas 19A (1st Floor) ☎ 218 882 841 🕙 Variable: check with tourist office for opening times 🚌 37; tram 28 💲 Inexpensive

Museum in a palace

The Palácio Pimenta provides the graceful setting for the Museu da Cidade. Built in the 18th century, during the reign of the free-spending Dom João V, the palace is distinguished by its *azulejos*. In the kitchen, these depict fish, swans, hares, and other creatures hung upside down on the walls. In the upstairs rooms, a ring of dado tiles describes each room's original function.

MUSEU DA MÚSICA

A collection of musical instruments from around Europe dating from the 16th to 20th centuries.
✚ E3 ✉ Rua Azinhaga do Ramalho ☎ 217 788 074 🕓 Tue–Sun 1:30–8 🚇 Alto dos Moihos 💷 Inexpensive. Under 14s free.

Vasco da Gama in the Discovery Room of the Museu Nacional Militar

MUSEU NACIONAL MILITAR

The National Military Museum is on the site of a 16th-century shipyard, later a naval foundry and store. Following a fire and the 1755 earthquake, the complex was rebuilt as an arsenal, becoming the Artillery Museum in 1851. Today, as well as an artillery collection —one of the world's best—the museum also has extensive displays of guns, pistols, and swords. Among them are Portuguese pieces dating back to the 16th century, together with artifacts of French, Dutch, English, Spanish, and Arab origin. Other highlights include the armory, paintings on military themes, and large spreads of tiles portraying battle scenes.
✚ K8 ✉ Caminhos de Ferro-Largo do Museu da Artilharia ☎ 218 842 569 🕓 Tue–Sun 10–5 🚌 9, 28, 39, 46 💷 Moderate. Free Wed

Puppet politics

Puppets in Portugal have been used for many years as powerful tools of political satire and subversion. They became especially popular during the 18th century, when puppet operas were used to poke fun at and explore the social and political affairs of the day. During the Salazar dictatorship, they were banned altogether.

MUSEU NACIONAL DO TEATRO

The National Theater Museum concentrates on the personalities who have graced the Lisbon stage over the years, which makes it of limited interest to the casual visitor. It is worth a look if you are visiting the neighboring Costume Museum, though, as it also has theatrical costumes, props, photographs, stage designs, and other theatrical ephemera.
✚ F1 ✉ Parque de Monteiro-Mor, Estrada do Lumiar 10 ☎ 217 567 410 🕓 Wed–Sun 10–6; Tue 2–6 (closes at 5 in winter). Closed public hols 🚌 1,3, 4, 7, 36, 101, 108 💷 Moderate; joint ticket with Museo Nacional do Traje

MUSEU NACIONAL DO TRAJE

The National Museum of Costume occupies the tiled and frescoed Palácio do Duque de Palmela, also known as the Palácio Monteiro-Mor, in the Parque do Monteiro-Mor at Lumiar, a northern suburb. Visit for the grounds and Jardim Botânico, dotted with pools, plants, and trees in a rugged hilly setting, as well as for the museum itself, which has beautiful old tapestries, jewels, toys, and costumes.
✚ F1 ✉ Parque de Monteiro-Mor, Largo Júlio de Castilho ☎ 217 590 318 🕓 Tue–Sun 10–6 (closes at 5 in winter) 🚌 1, 3, 4, 7 36, 101, 108 💷 Moderate; joint ticket with Museo Nacional do Teatro

VIEWS

CASTELO DE SÃO JORGE

The castle's walkways and terraces, and the castle parade in particular, provide the finest viewpoints, offering a cityscape dominated by the Mar de Palha, or "Straw Sea," the local name for the River Tagus. The view is best at sunset.

🗺 J8; cIII ✉ Rua Costa do Castelo 🚇 Rossio 🚌 37; tram 28

MIRADOURO DE SÃO PEDRO DE ALCÂNTARA

Perched on the edge of the Bairro Alto, this belvedere offers sweeping views of the Rossio and Baixa below. Part of the fun of coming up here is to travel the old Elevador da Glória, built in 1885, which lumbers up from just behind the tourist office in Praça dos Restauradores.

🗺 H7; all ✉ Rua São Pedro de Alcântara 🚇 Restauradores 🚌 58, 100; tram 24 or Gloria elevator

MIRADOURO DE SANTA LUZIA

This little area was laid out specially as a viewpoint (*miradouro* in Portuguese). The panorama extends across old rooftops—dotted with church towers—and down to the harbor and river beyond.

🗺 J8; cIII ✉ Largo de Santa Luzia 🚇 Rossio 🚌 37; tram 28

PONTE 25 DE ABRIL

Lisbon's 1-mile suspension bridge is a long way to go just for a view, but if you are driving from the south, you will cross it. The panorama embraces not only the broad span of the River Tagus, but also a large part of the old city, ranging from the Torre de Belém close at hand to the more distant quarters of the Alfama and Baixa. The bridge is notorious for traffic jams.

🗺 E10 ✉ Avenida da Ponte 🚇 Alcântara 🚌 52, 53

More viewpoints

The Santa Justa elevator (🗺 H8; bIII) gives a close-up of the Baixa. Largo de Santo Estêvão in the Alfama (🗺 J8) has views of the river, across rooftops crowded with TV aerials. Try the Miradouro da Nossa Senhora do Monte (🗺 K7), north of Campo de Santa Clara (➤ 46); the Miradouro da Santa Catarina (🗺 H8), in the Bairro Alto; and Parque Eduardo VII (🗺 G6, ➤ 58), whose northern flanks overlook the old city. The Torre de Belém (🗺 B10, ➤ 24) and ferries (➤ 19 and 59) give views of and from the river.

Lisbon seen from the Castelo de São Jorge

CHURCHES

Igreja de Santa Engrácia

St. Antony

Although St. Vincent is patron saint of Lisbon, St. Antony of Padua is the city's "unofficial" patron saint, as well as the much-venerated patron saint of Portugal. He is buried in Padua, but was born Fernando de Bulhoês in Lisbon, where the church of Santo Antonio de Lisboa now stands. The saint is revered as a matchmaker, protector of young brides, and patron of the lost and found. His feast day, wildly celebrated in Lisbon, is June 12 (▶ 22).

SANTO ANTÓNIO DE LISBOA

This little church stands on the site of the house where St. Antony was born in 1195. Built after the 1755 earthquake, it contains paintings by Pedro de Carvalho, who was responsible for the decoration of many churches after the disaster. The square in which the church and the cathedral are situated is called Santo António de Sé because the church is immediately in front of the cathedral. A small museum displays objects related to the saint's life.
➕ J8; bIII ✉ Largo de Santo António de Sé 24 ☎ 218 860 447 🕐 Museum Tue–Sun 10–1, 2–6. Closed public hols 🚌 37; tram 28 ♿ Inexpensive

SANTA ENGRÁCIA

The church of Santa Engrácia lies in the Alfama close to São Vicente de Fora. It is the Panteão Nacional, or National Pantheon. The large baroque building was begun in 1682, survived the 1755 earthquake, but was not completed until 1966 (when the cupola was finally added). The fact that this project took 284 years to complete has led to a little Portuguese idiom —*obras de Santa Engrácia*—used as a synonym for delayed or unfinished work. The early design (by João Antunes) centers on a balanced Greek Cross with four towers and curving arms, and was influenced by new departures in Italian baroque architecture of the period. The result is a slightly chill and over-precise building, its appearance well suited to its memorial function. Among the people buried here are the several Portuguese presidents, the poets Guerra Junqueiro and João de Deus, and writer Almeida Garrett, one of Portugal's leading 19th-century literary figures (the Chiado's Rua Garrett is named in his honor).
➕ K8 ✉ Campo de Santa Clara ☎ 218 128 419 🕐 Tue–Sun 10–5 🚌 12, 34, 104, 105, 107; tram 28 ♿ Inexpensive. Free Sun

SANTA LUZIA

The reasons for visiting this modest church are outside the building. Its exterior walls have *azulejos* depicting Lisbon before and after the earthquake of 1755, and its garden is laid out as a charming viewpoint, the Miradouro de Santa Luzia (▶ 53).
➕ J8; cIII ✉ Largo de Santa Luzia 🚇 Rossio 🚌 37; tram 28

NOSSA SENHORA DA CONCEIÇAO VELHA

Like Santa Luzia, this is one to enjoy from the outside. Most of the church collapsed in 1755, but the south doorway survived as a fine and rare exmple of the Manueline style—the ornate form of gothic associated with the reign of Manuel I (1495–1521) when wealth poured into Portugal.

✚ J8 ✉ Rua da Alfândega 🚌 104, 105; tram 15, 25, 28

SÃO VICENTE DE FORA

"St. Vincent Outside the Walls" was indeed outside the city walls when it was built between 1582 and 1627, over the site of a 12th-century church erected to commemorate the Crusaders' victory over the Moors. The construction of the present church took place during Portugal's period of subjugation to the Spanish, and was the work of Philip II of Spain's principal architect, the Italian Filippo Terzi. His cupola was felled by the 1755 earthquake and has been replaced by a more modest dome, though the majestic nave survives, its highlights a glorious coffered vault and extravagant baroque altar. The monastery and cloisters (through a gate to the right of the facade) are adorned with lovely 18th-century *azulejos* depicting rustic, court, and hunting scenes from La Fontaine's Fables. Off the cloisters the former refectory serves as Portugal's Royal Pantheon, which since 1855 has housed the tombs of most of the country's Bragança kings and queens from Dom João IV (died 1656) to Dom Carlos (assassinated 1908). The large *azulujo* panel depicts the taking of Lisbon from the Moors in 1147.

✚ J8, cll ✉ Rua Voz do Operário-Rua São Vicente ☎ 218 824 400 🕐 Tue–Sun 10–6 🚌 12; tram 28 🎟 Church free. Monastery inexpensive

St. Vincent

When São Vicente, or St. Vincent, was martyred in Valencia, his body was taken by boat, reputedly under the guidance of two ravens, to the desolate headland in southwest Portugal now known as Cabo de São Vicente (Cape St. Vincent). The ravens were seen again in 1173, when the saint's relics were removed to Lisbon on the orders of Afonso Henriques, Portugal's founding king. Vincent became the city's patron saint, and the ravens appear in the city's crest.

The tiled sacristy of São Vicente de Fora

PARKS & GARDENS

Walk up the avenue

Avenida da Liberdade cuts a 1,350-yard, tree-lined swathe from the Rossio north to the Praça Marquês de Pombal junction, where Parque Eduardo VII begins. This is Lisbon's grandest road, and inevitably invites comparison with the Champs Elysées in Paris. Though no peaceful green oasis, it is well worth a stroll for its trees, water features, pavement mosaics, 19th-century buildings, and outdoor cafés.

A fountain in the Jardim Guerra Junqueiro—the Jardim da Estrela

CASTELO DE SÃO JORGE

The highlights of Lisbon's ancient citadel are the views from its ramparts and the lovely expanses of lawns and gardens laid out in and around its walls. Birds wander around, many of them exotic and most of them quite tame, while ducks and other waterfowl dive and dabble in the garden's many ponds and fountains. There are also plenty of benches and picnic tables.

✚ J8; cIII ⊠ Rua Costa do Castelo ◷ Apr–Sep: daily 9–9. Oct–Mar: daily 9–7 🚌 37; tram 12, 28 ♿ Free

JARDIM BOTÂNICO

Lisbon's principal botanical gardens lie across a hilly slope just above the busy Avenida da Liberdade. An oasis of calm in frantic surroundings, they are—with the Parque Eduardo VII and Castelo de São Jorge gardens—the areas of green space you should make a special point of seeing if your time in the city is limited. Laid out in 1873, they are still the responsibility of the Faculdade das Ciências (Faculty of Sciences), whose slightly decrepit building you pass on the main way in, along a palm-lined alley. Mazes of little paved paths wind downhill, wending their way past masses of exotic plants and trees (some 10,000 plants in total), all clearly labeled. A couple of small, fish-filled lakes enhance the scene. The back entrance on Rua da Algeria is closed on weekends.

✚ H7 ⊠ Rua Escola Politécnica-Rua da Alegria ☎ 213 921 800 ◷ Daily 9–6 🚇 Avenida/Rato 🚌 58, 100 ♿ Free

JARDIM GUERRA JUNQUEIRO

This easy-going park is better known locally as the Jardim da Estrela after the Basílica da Estrela (➤ 32), which lies immediately to the south. A neighborhood park, it is a favorite among mothers and children, with plenty of specially designated areas for kids to play in. Adults can sit and watch the goings-on from the comfort of shaded benches. There are elm and plane trees, with little enclosed flower-beds providing patches of color, and a small duck-dotted lake (with a nice adjacent café), which serves as the park's natural focus. There is also an attractive wrought-iron gazebo, and on summer afternoons you may be lucky enough to catch one of the occasional brass band concerts.

✚ G7–G8 ⊠ Calçada da Estrela ◷ 7–midnight 🍴 Café 🚇 Rato 🚌 9, 20, 22, 26, 27, 38; tram 25, 28 ♿ Free

JARDIM ZOOLÓGICO DE LISBOA

Lisbon's zoo (▶ 60) may be somewhat lackluster, but it has an appealing setting in the former Parque das Laranjeiras, an old estate whose rose gardens, ponds, and formal flower-beds have been carefully preserved among the animals. The upper, northern part of the park is wilder and less cultivated, offering places for picnics and leisurely exploration, although you do have to pay to go into the zoo itself. In particular the Miradouro dos Moinhos (the Mill Belvedere) provides a broad panorama across much of the Monsanto park and the rest of the city. The park also has an eccentric little cemetery for dogs.

✚ F4 ✉ Estrada de Benfica 158–60–Parque dos Laranjeiras ☎ 217 232 900 ⏱ Summer: daily 10–8. Winter: daily 10–6 🍴 Café 🚇 Sete Rios 🚌 16, 26, 31, 41, 46, 54, 55, 58, 68 💷 Expensive

PALÁCIO DOS MARQUÊSES DE FRONTEIRA

This wonderful palace (▶ 30) lies in the northeast corner of the Parque Florestal de Monsanto (see ▶ 58), secreted away amid lovely gardens that provide a buffer against the rather ugly modern neighborhood nearby with its concrete and traintracks. Although laid out to an Italian Renaissance plan, the gardens' vast numbers of *azulejos* (decorative tiles) give them an unmistakably Portuguese flavor. Virtually every possible patch of wall, terrace, and fountain has been adorned with tiles, their blues and greens complementing the natural colors of water, trees, and plants.

✚ E5 ✉ Largo de São Domingos de Benfica 1 ☎ 21 778 2023 ⏱ Times change regularly; call for latest details 🚇 Sete Rios 🚌 72 💷 Moderate

Topiary in the garden of the Fronteira Palace

Cats

The Palácio dos Marquêses de Fronteira has some striking cats among its exterior tile decorations. This is apt for Lisbon, which has a big population of cats, many of them feral but fed by local people, who tend to be well disposed towards their feline neighbors.

Cool and hot

The Estufa Fria (Cool House) at Parque Eduardo VII has humid and perfumed halls filled with exotic flowers, shrubs, and trees from across the globe. Numerous pathways weave past indoor ponds, fountains, streams, and waterfalls, all full of fish, statues, and pretty stones. The Estufa Quente (Hot House) opens off the Estufa Fria and has many of the same features, but here the plants and temperatures are tropical and the air is filled with the twitter of bird song. Off the Hot House is a Cactus House crammed with many hundreds of exotic cacti of all shapes and sizes.

PARQUE EDUARDO VII

Lisbon's foremost park is Parque Eduardo VII, which lies at the northern end of the grand Avenida da Liberdade. Officially opened in 1902, it was named in honor of King Edward VII of Britain, who visited Portugal that year to reconfirm the age-old Anglo-Portuguese alliance (first signed in 1386). The park centers on two broad, mosaic-paved boulevards, which in turn are intersected by tiny walkways and carefully manicured little hedgerows. Off to the east lies the large neo-baroque Pavilhão dos Desportos, a sports pavilion recently repainted and renamed in honor of the Olympic marathon champion Carlos Lopes. Its tile panels depict battle scenes from Portugal's wars of independence against the Moors and Spanish. There are panoramic views from Rua Alamada Cardeal Cerejeira on the northern side, and wonderful cool and hot houses, lovely places to spend a tranquil half an hour away from the city's fuss and fumes (see panel this page).

🚇 G6 ✉ Praça Marquês de Pombal ☎ Cool and hot houses 213 882 278 🕐 Cool and hot houses: Apr–Sep: daily 9–6. Oct–Mar: daily 9–5 🍴 Café 🚇 Parque, Marquês de Pombal or São Sebastião 🚌 1, 2, 12, 20, 22, and many other services to Praça Marquês de Pombal ♿ Park free. Cool and hot houses inexpensive

PARQUE FLORESTAL DE MONSANTO

This enormous area of parkland on the western fringes of Lisbon is probably the city's most positive legacy of Salazar, but it is not recommended for walking. It is poorly kept and overgrown—its size makes maintenance a problem—and some parts are distinctly dangerous and insalubrious by day or night. Furthermore, the prominent Forte de Monsanto is used as a prison. However, if you have transportation it is worth visiting for the public tennis courts, the running track, and the children's playground, and there are fine views from the Miradouro de Monsanto and Miradouro dos Montes Claros.

🚇 A5–E5–9 ✉ West of Avenida de Ceuta 🕐 Always open ♿ Free

Strelitzia in the Parque Eduardo VII

FREE SIGHTS

OLD DISTRICTS

Lisbon is such an inexpensive city relative to most western European capitals that it is hard to begrudge the almost universally low admission charges to many of its key sights. It also has a feast of pleasures that require no outlay save a little time. Chief among these is wandering in the city's older quarters—the Bairro Alto (➤ 35), Chiado (➤ 37), Baixa (➤ 40) and Alfama (➤ 44).

CHURCHES

There is no charge for visiting Lisbon's many ornate churches, although you may be required to pay a small fee to see areas such as the treasury. The most notable churches are the Igreja de São Roque (➤ 36), the Sé (cathedral, ➤ 42), and Igreja da Madre de Deus (➤ 47).

VIEWS

Lisbon has several named *miradouros* and other viewpoints (➤ 53), and you will find others by just wandering. City views can be had for next to nothing by crossing the River Tagus on one of the ferries from the Cais de Alfândega on the main Praça do Comércio, especially if you then take a ride to the top of the Cristo Rey statute. There are three basic crossings: to Calcilhas, Barreiro, and Montijo. Tickets are very inexpensive, and views of the river and city are superb on all three routes. You could also make a ferry-boat trip from Belém, from where services run to Trafaria.

Old streets run down from the heights

Watch your step

Walking about is a must in Lisbon. As well as the *azulejos* that brighten the facades of numerous buildings (➤ 48), you will also see mosaics set into the pavements. Cobbled streets, steps, and steep hills are hard on the feet, so wear comfortable shoes for your explorations.

SQUARES AND PARKS

For the price of a drink you can sit at an outside café in one of Lisbon's great squares and watch the world go by. The Rossio (➤ 39) and Praça dos Restauradores spring most readily to mind. Or find a more intimate perch in one of the old-world cafés in the Chiado or Bairro Alto (➤ 69). You can retreat from the streets to green spaces such as the Parque Eduardo VII and the gardens around the castle (➤ 56–58), or the gardens, round the Gulbenkian Museum (➤ 33). Browsing Lisbon's street markets and flea market (➤ 46) is excellent free entertainment—unless you are tempted by a "bargain." The best street market is to be found at the Campo de Santa Clara.

ATTRACTIONS FOR CHILDREN

Parque das Nações

Built for the '98 Expo, this site in east Liston offers many attractions that will appeal to children. Apart from the Oceanário (► see this page), you can take a ride up the Vasco da Gama tower for excellent views over the city, River Tagus and Vasco da Gama Bridge or you can view the whole expo site from the Lisbon Cable Car (🚩 M2 ☎ 218 965 416 🕐 Tower daily; cable car Mon–Fri 11–7 🚇 Oriente).

Lisbon for children

Sights such as the Torre de Belém (► 24), the children's museum in the Museu de Marinha (► 25), and Museu dos Coches (► 29) are likely to appeal to children. Other pastimes include a visit to the Feira Popular, the big funfair held in the north of the city center from June to September; a ride on a tram; and boat trips (► 19, 59).

CASTELO DE BRINCAR

This tiny medieval castle-within-a-castle, in the Castelo de São Jorge, is full of slides, swings, and ropes for children to play on.
🚩 J8, cIII ✉ Rua Costa do Castelo 🕐 Apr–Sep: daily 9–9. Oct–Mar: daily 9–7 🚋 37; tram 12, 28 ♿ Poor 🎟 Free

JARDIM ZOOLÓGICO DE LISBOA

Lisbon's zoo, home to some 2,000 animals (350 species), has long been underfunded with some enclosures appearing stark compared to some of its European counterparts. However, it claims Europe's best dolphinarium, and the dolphin shows, cable car, and rowing boats for rent may appeal to children. The lovely garden is a pleasure to explore (► 57). Northwest of the city center (close to a subway stop) it's best visited in conjunction with the nearby Palácio dos Marquêses de Fronteira (► 30, 57).
🚩 F4 ✉ Estrada de Benfica 158–160-Parque das Laranjeiras ☎ 217 232 900 🕐 Summer: daily 9–8. Winter: daily 9–6 🍽 Café 🚇 Sete Rios 🚌 16, 26, 31, 41, 54, 58, 68 🎟 Expensive

OCEANÁRIO

Spectacularly designed by Peter Chermayeff, this is Europe's largest oceanarium. Opened in 1998, as part of Expo '98, it is home to water species from the five different oceans. The vast central tank is surrounded by four smaller tanks with two viewing levels.
🚩 M2 ✉ Praça das Nações ☎ 218 965 416 🕐 Daily 10–7 🚇 Oriente 🎟 Expensive

PLANETÁRIO CALOUSTE GULBENKIAN

Sponsored by the Gulbenkian Foundation, the Planetarium is an annex of the Museu de Marinha and has special children's shows.

🚩 B9 ✉ Praça do Império ☎ 213 620 002 🕐 Children's performances Sat 4; Sun 11 and 4 🚇 Belém 🚌 29, 43, 49; tram 15 🎟 Moderate

LISBON
where to...

FINE DINING

Prices

Expect to pay per person for a meal excluding drinks:

$ under 3,000$00

$$ 3,000$00–6,000$00

$$$ over 6,000$00

Cover charge, taxes, and tips

Restaurants will often bring plates of starters such as bread, ham, cheeses, and olives. These will be charged to your bill as "couvert" or cover charge unless you send them back. Very few people do this as they are great and unless you are in a very fancy restaurant they will make little difference to the final bill. Value added tax or IVA is added to restaurant bills at 8 percent. Most bills say "IVA incluido" and already include this charge. Tips are welcomed and generally expected as a service charge is rarely included on the bill. Anything from 5 percent is considered acceptable.

ANTÓNIO CLARA ($$$)

Polished wood, antiques, and gilded mirrors set off the fine art nouveau decor of the 19th-century villa in which the restaurant is set. Dress up and revel in the ambience. Specialties include smoked swordfish and monkfish rice.
🚇 H4 ✉ Avenida da República 38 ☎ 217 994 280 ⏰ Mon–Sat lunch, dinner ⓜ Entrecampos

AVIZ ($$$)

Located at the heart of the Chiado district, this is one of Lisbon's most stately and revered restaurants—clubby and old-fashioned, with lots of crystal, paintings, chandeliers, and leather armchairs.
🚇 H8 ✉ Rua Serpa Pinto 12b ☎ 213 851 888 ⏰ Mon–Fri lunch; dinner reservations only ⓜ Baixa-Chiado 🚊 Tram 28

BACHUS ($$$)

A popular and stylish restaurant. Especially good are the mixed-grill Bachus, mountain goat, and Bachus shrimp.
🚇 H8; alll ✉ Largo da Trindade 9 ☎ 213 421 260 ⏰ Mon–Fri lunch, dinner 🚊 58, 100

CASA DA COMIDA ($$$)

Among Lisbon's finest French-Portuguese restaurants, this is a good place to treat yourself, though it is well north-west of the city center. The setting is wonderful —a former mansion in a little square. In summer you can eat outside.
🚇 G7 ✉ Travessa das Amoireiras 1, off Rua Alexandre Herculano ☎ 213 859 386 ⏰ Mon–Fri lunch, dinner; Sat dinner ⓜ Rato 🚊 12, 18, 42, 51

COLARES VELHO ($$$)

If you are staying in the Sintra area and want to be sure of an excellent meal, it is worth driving out to Colares (about 10 minutes drive to the west) to this excellent little restaurant. Try the monkfish in garlic and coriander sauce.
🚇 off map ✉ Largo Dr. Carlos França, 1-4 Colares Sintra ☎ 219 292 406 ⏰ Tue–Sun lunch, dinner

CONFRARIA AT YORK HOUSE ($$$)

Tucked away in a 17th-century former carmelite convent, this restaurant with its oasis-like courtyard has transformed its cuisine over the last few years. An extensive selection of traditional Portuguese dishes served with refined elegance.
🚇 G8 ✉ Rue das Janelas Verdes 32 ☎ 213 962 435 ⏰ Daily lunch, dinner 🚊 24, 40, 49, 60; tram 25

CONVENTUAL ($$-$$$)

This restaurant is finely decorated with antique and modern religious art and the famous Arraiolos carpets. Its religious theme continues in the names of its dishes: pope of Avignon snails, and in its excellent *doces conventuais* tradition, sweet, eggy desserts originally made by nuns.
🚇 G7–G8 ✉ Praça das Flores 45 ☎ 213 909 196

◉ Mon–Fri lunch, dinner; Sat dinner only. Closed Aug ⊠ Rato, Avenida 🚌 100

O NOBRE ($$$)

A favorite among top politicians, this small and perhaps a little cramped establishment offers crab soup served in its own shell, partridge stuffed with fois-gras, and truffles cooked in port.

✚ C9 ⊠ Rue das Mercês 71A/B ☎ 213 633 827 ◉ Mon–Fri lunch, dinner; Sat dinner only 🚌 14, 73

RESTAURANTE 33 ($$-$$$)

Conveniently located for many of the Avenida hotels and decorated in the style of an English hunting lodge, this restaurant specializes in a range of dishes including smoked salmon, lobster, or pepper steak. Live piano music will often accompany your meal.

✚ G7–G8 ⊠ Rua Alexandre Herculano 33A ☎ 213 546 079 ◉ Mon–Fri lunch, dinner; Sat dinner only ⊠ Marquês de Pombal 🚌 6, 74

SUA EXCÊLENCIA ($$-$$$)

Worth a visit if in the Lapa district. This restaurant is renowned for its innovative Angolan and Mozambican influenced Portuguese cuisine. Dishes include prawns in the Mozambique style, and an Angolan chicken dish. Reservation essential.

✚ F8 ⊠ Rua do Conde 34 ☎ 213 903 614 ◉ Mon, Tues, Thu, Fri lunch; dinner; Sat, Sun dinner. Closed Sep 🚌 27, 49; tram 25

TÁGIDE ($$$)

A very elegant restaurant up from the waterfront on a hilltop in the Chiado district. Tiled portraits of Portuguese queens punctuate the white-washed walls, and chandeliers hang above. Reserve early to secure a window table with lovely views over the port and city. Specialties include stuffed crab and cold orange and lemon soufflé with hot chocolate sauce.

✚ H8 ⊠ Largo Académia Nacional de Belas Artes 18–20 ☎ 213 420 720 ◉ Mon–Fri lunch, dinner ⊠ Baixa-Chiado 🚌 58, 100; tram 15, 28

TAVARES ($$$)

For years this glittering old-world establishment, founded as a café in 1784, had a reputation as the best of Lisbon's grand old restaurants. It still attracts politicians, diplomats, and the literary set.

✚ H8; all ⊠ Rua da Misericórdia 35–37 ☎ 213 421 112 ◉ Mon–Fri lunch, dinner ⊠ Baixa-Chiado 🚌 Tram 15, 28

VELA LATINA ($$$)

This light, airy, and tastefully decorated restaurant can boast one of Lisbon's prime locations as it stands on the waterfront beside the Torre de Belém. Don't get the restaurant confused with the popular self-service restaurant at the front of the complex. The chef mixes national and international cuisine.

✚ B10 ⊠ Doca Bom Sucesso ☎ 213 017 118 ◉ Mon–Sat lunch, dinner 🚌 29; tram 15

Practicalities

The Portuguese eat earlier than their Spanish neighbors. Lunch runs from around 12:30 to 2:30, while dinner lasts from 7:30 to 10:30. Some restaurants close all day Sunday and on Saturday lunchtime. Some also close on Wednesday. The menu in Portuguese is known as the *lista* or *ementa*. An *ementa turística* is not a tourist menu, but the menu of the day. It usually offers a modest choice, and often represents excellent value, especially in inexpensive restaurants. The dish of the day is the *prato do dia*. Eating à la carte is *à lista*.

Most Fashionable

Booking

These restaurants are currently among Lisbon's most "happening." If you want to join the "in" crowd to see what all the fuss is about you must reserve early to avoid disapointment.

A CHARCUTARIA ($$–$$$)

Originally opening just for friends, demand grew and eventually this restaurant was opened to the public. It specializes in Alentejan dishes such as *açorda* (bread soup) and *migas* (fried bread and pork).

✚ H8 ✉ Rua do Alecrim 47 ☎ 213 423 845 🕐 Mon–Fri lunch, dinner; Sat–Sun dinner only Ⓜ Cais do Sodré 🚌 58, 100

BICA DO SAPATO ($$–$$$)

Recently opened by the same owner as the ever popular Pap'Açorda (► 65), Bicado Sapato has become Lisbon's ultimate trendy restaurant. With its super modern interior of wood, glass, and chrome, views over the river, and excellent sushi, it has been praised both at home and abroad.

✚ K8 ✉ Av. Infante D. Henrique, Armazem B ☎ 218 810 320 🕐 Tue–Sat lunch, dinner; Sun dinner only 🚌 9, 12, 46, 90

CAFÉ DA LAPA ($$)

Joaquim Figueiredo is perhaps Portugal's best known in international circles. Having grown up in France, his cooking blends traditional Portuguese dishes and ingredients with French nouvelle cusine.

✚ G8 ✉ Rue São João da Mata 30-32 ☎ 213 962 683 🕐 Tue–Sun dinner only 🚌 27 tram 25

ESPAÇO LISBOA ($$–$$$)

It is worth eating here just for the architecture. Housed in an old factory building, this huge restaurant is decorated with thousands of beautiful tiles. Espaço Lisboa specializes in Portuguese cooking.

✚ E9 ✉ Rua da Cozinha Económica 16 ☎ 213 610 212 🕐 Wed–Mon lunch, dinner Ⓜ Alcântara–Cascais line from Cais do Sodré 🚌 38; tram 15, 18

LA VILLA ($$–$$$)

On the waterfront at Estoril, this is an excellent choice if you want to get out of central Lisbon and dine above the beach. La Villa serves excellent sushi and specializes in nouvelle cuisine.

✚ off map ✉ Praia do Estoril ☎ 214 680 033 🕐 Daily lunch, dinner Ⓜ Estoril–Cascais line from Cais do Sodré

SOLAR DOS NUNES ($$)

This small restaurant features game, including wild boar, partridge, and hare in season. Also excellent value steaks.

✚ E9–8 ✉ Rua dos Lusiadas 68–72 ☎ 213 647 359 or 213 631 631 🕐 Mon–Sat lunch, dinner 🚌 22; tram 18, 15

XL ($$–$$$)

The ocre-painted walls, rustic furniture, and antique curiosities give this extremely popular restaurant a cozy, homey feel. Camembert in bread crumbs with raspberry sauce and soufflés, are their forte.

✚ G8 ✉ Calçada da Estrela 57 ☎ 213 956 118 🕐 Mon–Sat dinner only 🚌 6,13, 39, 49, 100; tram 28

REGIONAL & TRADITIONAL

BOTA ALTA ($)

An attractive and rustic restaurant in the Bairro Alto. The big portions and traditional cooking draw crowds.

➕ H7; all ✉ Travessa da Queimada 35 ☎ 213 427 959 ⏰ Mon–Fri lunch, dinner; Sat dinner only 🚇 Restauradores–Elevador da Glória or Baixa-Chiado 🚌 58; tram 28

CASA DO ALENTEJO ($$)

This restaurant, set in a 19th-century Franco-Arabic style building with wonderful tiles, is a celebration of the Alentejo region as much as of the Alentejan cuisine. There is often folk dancing on Saturdays.

➕ H7; all ✉ Praça Santo Antão-Rua das Portas de Santo Antão 58 ☎ 213 475 055 ⏰ Tue–Sun lunch, dinner 🚇 Restauradores

LAUTASCO ($$)

This restaurant in the Alfama is popular with visitors and locals who come here not so much for the food, which is simple Portuguese fare, but for the delightful atmospheric courtyard.

➕ J8; cIII ✉ Beco do Azinhal 7, off Rua de São Pedro-Largo Chafariz de Dentro ☎ 218 860 173 ⏰ Mon–Sat lunch, dinner 🚌 104, 105

O POLEIRO ($$)

Opened in 1985, this family-run restaurant offers traditional cusine in a simple but friendly environment.

➕ H4 ✉ Rua de Entrecampos 30-A ☎ 217 976 265 ⏰ Mon–Fri lunch, dinner; Sat dinner only 🚇 Campo Pequeno/Entrecampos

PAP'AÇORDA ($$)

Trendy, predominantly young and arty clientele frequent this restaurant in a converted bakery. Try the *açorda* (bread soup).

➕ H8; aIII ✉ Rua da Atalaia 57–9 ☎ 213 464 811 ⏰ Tue–Sat lunch, dinner 🚇 Baixa-Chiado 🚌 58, 100; tram 28

PORTA BRANCA ($$)

A good choice if you want to try authentic national cooking. It specializes in favorite Portuguese dishes such as *bacalhau* (salt cod) and *arroz de pato* (rice with duck).

➕ H8; all-III ✉ Rua do Teixeira 35 ☎ 213 421 024 ⏰ Mon–Fri lunch, dinner; Sat dinner. Closed Jul 🚇 Restauradores–Elevador da Glória 🚌 58, 100

RESTAURANTE MALMEQUER-BEMMEQUER ($–$$)

A welcoming choice in an evocative street in the Alfama district. Plenty of basic Portuguese dishes.

➕ J8; cIII ✉ Rua São Miguel 23–5, Largo de São Miguel ☎ 218 876 535 ⏰ Wed–Sun lunch, dinner; Tue dinner

VIA GRAÇA ($$–$$$)

This candlelit restaurant, with a romantic city view, is in the hilly reaches of the Graça district to the northeast of the Castelo de São Jorge. Cooking is traditional Portuguese.

➕ J7; cI ✉ Rua Damasceno Monteiro 98 ☎ 218 870 830 ⏰ Mon–Fri, lunch, dinner; Sat dinner 🚇 Intendente 🚌 Tram 28

Basics

Hors d'ouevres are *acepipes*. Breakfast is *pequeno almoço*, lunch *almoço*, and dinner *jantar*. Soups are typically inexpensive and filling as a first course. Meat (*carne*) and poultry (*aves*) are usually simply grilled or fried: roast or barbecued chicken is a particularly tasty Portuguese specialty. Fish (*peixe*) and seafood (*mariscos*), though, are preeminent in Lisbon. Salt cod (*bacalhau*) and sardines (*sardinhas*) are virtually the national dishes. Vegetables are *legumes* and salad *salada*. Bread is *pão*.

Tascas

Portugal's traditional eating haunts are known as *tascas* from the old word *tascar* to eat. A *tasca* offers no frills, just good honest traditional fare whose cooking and poorman's recipes uses bread, pork bits, and whatever the earth provided for them. Portions are huge and prices very reasonable. This food is known as *comida regional*, though not relating to any particular region but rather to the country as a whole. It's the same as *comida tipic*, i.e. typically Portuguese.

SEAFOOD

Port

Port is a Douro region wine that is sweet because brandy has been added at a certain point to stop the grape sugar turning into alcohol. It may be red or white. Young red port, or *tinto*, is the most common, and is distinctive and highly fruity. Reds are used to make "blended" ports, the blend comprising ports from different years, the quality depending on the wines used. Reds are also the basis of vintage, ruby and tawny ports (see panels below and opposite). White port, or *branco*, is sometimes fermented again to remove the sweetness. If chilled, this dry white port makes a delicious apéritif.

Ruby and tawny

Ruby, or *tinto-aloirado*, is slightly older than *tinto*, hence its different color, and will often be blended from a variety of more aged ports. Tawny, or *aloirado*, is made from port that has aged longer in the cask (usually at least seven years), a process which imparts its distinctive golden-brown, or "tawny" color.

CAIS DA RIBEIRA ($$–$$$)

Housed in one of the many, now converted, warehouses along the dockside, this restaurant offers excellent fresh fish and seafood, and fine views of the River Tagus.
✚ H9 ⊠ Armazem A-2, Cais do Sodré ☎ 213 423 611 🕓 Mon–Fri lunch, dinner; Sat dinner only 🚇 Cais do Sodré 🚌 15, 18

CERVEJARIA PINÓQUIO ($$)

Established in the Baixa for over 30 years, this simple restaurant offers no frills. Diners sit at long tables, service is quick but the fish is fresh daily from Setúbal. If the sea is rough, supplies run low.
✚ H7; all ⊠ Praça dos Restauradores 79 ☎ 213 465 106 🕓 Daily lunch, dinner 🚇 Restauradores

FAZ FIGURA ($$)

This restaurant provides excellent service and fine views over the Tagus. The best on the menu includes *feijoada de marisco* (shellfish) and seafood *cataplana* (large round-bottomed copper dish).
✚ K8 ⊠ Rua do Paraíso 15B ☎ 218 868 981 🕓 Mon–Fri lunch, dinner; Sat dinner only 🚌 104, 105

FIDALGO ($–$$)

This popular rendezvous for media types is trendier than most of the Bairro Alto restaurants. Great fish.
✚ H8; all ⊠ Rua da Barroca 27 ☎ 213 422 900 🕓 Mon–Sat lunch, dinner 🚇 Baixa-Chiado 🚌 58, 100; tram 28

GAMBRINUS ($$$)

This restaurant, just off the Rossio, rivals Aviz (►62) for the title of Lisbon's most expensive restaurant, but here the culinary emphasis is on fish and seafood. The setting is suitably formal, with leather chairs and beamed ceiling. Reservations are essential.
✚ H7; all ⊠ 25 Rua das Portas de Santo Antão 23 ☎ 213 421 466 🕓 Daily lunch, dinner 🚇 Rossio/Restauradores

MERCADO DO PEIXE ($$$)

Perhaps one of Lisbon's more upmarket fish and seafood restaurants, it is well worth the trip out to Ajuda (just before Belém).
✚ C8 ⊠ Estrada de Casal Pedro Teixeira ☎ 213 623 140 🕓 Tue–Sat lunch, dinner; Sun lunch only 🚌 27, 29; tram 18

SOLMAR ($$)

In this big, busy, down-to-earth place in the Baxia district seafood is the specialty but there are also game dishes. Dine amid 1950s decor.
✚ H7; all ⊠ Rua das Portas de Sao Antão 108 ☎ 213 423 371 🕓 Daily lunch, dinner 🚇 Restauradores 🚌 1, 2, 9, 11, 31, Avenida da Liberdade services

RIBADOURO ($–$$)

Eat informally at the bar or go downstairs to the main restaurant for a full meal. Excellent seafood.
✚ H7 ⊠ Corner of Rua do Salitre and Avenida da Liberdade 155 ☎ 21 354 9411 🕓 Daily lunch, dinner 🚇 Avenida 🚌 1, 2, 9, 11, 31 and all other Avenida da Liberdade services

INTERNATIONAL

ESCORIAL ($$–$$$)

This wood paneled dining room in the center offers classic Spanish dishes such as roast kid or partridge casserole.

✚ H7; all ✉ Rua das Portas de Santo Antão 47 ☎ 213 464 429 🕐 Daily lunch, dinner 🚇 Restauradores

COMIDA DE SANTO ($$)

This lively Brazilian restaurant is known for its powerful cocktails and South American-influenced Portuguese dishes. Try the delicious *feijoada* (bean stew).

✚ G7 ✉ Calçada Engenheiro Miguel Pais 39, off Rua da Escola Politécnica ☎ 213 963 339 🕐 Daily lunch, dinner 🚌 58, 100

LYCHEE ($–$$)

Offering some of the best Chinese food in Lisbon, its dishes include honey-garlic chicken wings and shrimps in pepper sauce.

✚ H7 ✉ Rua Barata Salgueiro 37 ☎ 213 148 888 🕐 Daily lunch, dinner 🚇 Avenida or Marquês de Pombal 🚌 all Avenida da Liberdade services

MASSIMA CULPA ($$)

Spaghetti house offering a wide range of Italian pasta dishes with a young, lively atmosphere. Don't miss its champagne sangria.

✚ H8; alll ✉ Rua da Atalaia 35/37 ☎ 213 420 121 🕐 Thu–Tue dinner only 🚌 58, 100; tram 28

MEZZALUNA ($$)

Italian restaurant catering for a slightly older, quieter crowd than the Massima.

✚ G6 ✉ Rua Artilharia Um 16 ☎ 213 879 944 🕐 Mon–Fri lunch, dinner; Sat dinner only 🚇 Marquês de Pombal 🚌 11, 23, 48, 53

O CANTINHO DO AZIZ ($)

Informal and rather rough and ready, this is a great place to sample spicy Mozambique and Angolan cooking. A little hard to find: it is situated in the northwest corner of the Alfama district.

✚ J8; bll ✉ Rua de São Lourenço 3–5 ☎ 218 876 472 🕐 Mon–Sat lunch, dinner 🚇 Rossio/Martim Moniz

PICANHA ($$)

Excellent Brazilian grilled meats, *farofa* (manioc), *feijão* (beans), and other Brazilian delights. Try the *caipirinhas*, alcoholic lemon punches.

✚ G9–10 ✉ Rua das Janelas Verdes 96 ☎ 213 975 401 🕐 Mon–Fri lunch, dinner; Sat, Sun dinner only 🚌 27, 40, 49, 60; tram 25

ÚLTIMO TANGO ($–$$)

Located in the Bairro Alto, this Argentinian restaurant offers excellent steaks and a fine selection of Argentinian wines.

✚ H8; alll ✉ Rua Diário de Notícias 62 ☎ 213 420 341 🕐 Mon–Sat lunch, dinner 🚌 58, 100; tram 28

VELHA GÔA ($$)

Tasty Goanese cuisine, with mild to flaming hot curries; try the prawn chicken or Madrasta.

✚ F7 ✉ Rua Tomás da Anunciação 41 ☎ 213 900 446 🕐 Mon–Fri lunch, dinner; Sat dinner only 🚌 74, tram 25, 28

Colonial influence

Colonial days may be long gone but their inheritance lives on especially in Portugal's cuisine. As Portuguese returned from the ex-colonies they brought with them such dishes as *moamba* from Angola, *cachupa* from Caboverde, the typical tiger prawns grilled in *piri-piri* sauce from Mozambique. From Goa came the *chamuças* and curries and from Brazil the roast meats of the *picanha* and the famous bean feast known as *feijoada Brazilieira*.

All these and many more can now be found around the city, both in their own typical restaurants and dotted through the menus of traditionally Portuguese establishments, often opened by those who spent years abroad.

LIGHT MEALS

Half portions

Servings tend to be generous in Portugal, and many soups and appetizers are rich and filling enough to be meals in themselves. If you can't manage whole portions, ask if you can have a half portion, or share one serving between two—many restaurants are happy to serve smaller portions, especially those in the lower price range, and some even list half portions on the menu.

With children

Eating out with children should not be a problem—it is common to see even very young children out with their parents late at night. Restaurants are welcoming and serve half portions, or are happy to let young children share their parents' meals.

Cervejarias

Cervejarias or beer houses are a great option when looking for a quick, light meal. With a limited menu offering steaks with fries, prawns, and of course beer, these are like Portugal's "fast food" restaurants, serving into the early hours.

ALFAIA ($)
A busy and popular restaurant, especially for lunch. You need search no further for a reasonably priced meal in a typically Bairro Alto establishment.
✚ H8; allI ✉ Travessa da Queimada 18–24 ☎ 213 461 232 ⊙ Tue–Sat, lunch, dinner; Mon lunch ⊖ Restauradores

BOMDIA ($)
These two Bomdia cafés/restaurants offer snacks and light meals in informal surroundings.
✚ H7 ✉ Rua Rodrigues Sampaio 76 ☎ 213 541 339 ⊙ Daily ⊖ Avenida ⊟ All Avenida Liberdade services;
✚ H8; allI ✉ Rua da Misercórdia 78 ☎ 213 541 339 ⊙ Daily ⊖ Baixa-Chiado ⊟ 58, 100

BONJARDIM ($–$$)
This Lisbon institution, with three outlets on the same street, appeals to all tastes and budgets. The downstairs dining room is lined with tiles; upstairs the decor is wood-beamed.
✚ H7; all ✉ Travesa de Santo Antão 10–11 ☎ 213 427 424 or 213 424 389 ⊙ Daily lunch, dinner ⊖ Restauradores

CAFÉ NO CHIADO ($–$$)
Restored 18th-century building filled with modern furnishings serving steak and fries to a young, artistic crowd.
✚ H8; all ✉ Largo do Picadeiro 11–12 ☎ 213 424 517 ⊙ Daily lunch, dinner ⊖ Baixa-Chiado ⊟ 58, 100

CASA FAZ FRIO ($)
Located on the northern edge of the Bairro Alto, this is one of Lisbon's lovelier and more traditional restaurants. Known for its low prices and good seafood.
✚ H7 ✉ Rua Dom Pedro V 96 ☎ 213 461 860 ⊙ Daily lunch, dinner ⊖ Restauradores–Elevador da Glória ⊟ 58, 100

CERVEJARIA TRINDADE ($–$$)
This large beer hall and azulejo-lined restaurant in a former convent in the Chiado is one of the city's oldest eating places in business since 1836. The food is nothing special, but the place is a classic, and a fun spot to visit.
✚ H8; allI ✉ Rua Nova da Trindade 20b ☎ 213 423 506 ⊙ Daily until 2AM ⊖ Baixa-Chiado ⊟ 20, 24, 100; tram 28, 58

ENOTECA ($$)
Housed in the beautiful 18th-century building known as the "Chafariz do Vinho," it's an excellent place for a tapas style plate of ham, spicey sausage, and cheeses, plus a glass of wine.
✚ H7 ✉ Rua da Mâe d' Água à Praça da Alegria ☎ 213 422 079 ⊙ Tue–Sun dinner only from 6PM ⊖ Restauradores–Elevador da Glória ⊟ 58, 100

PORTUGÁLIA RIO ($$)
One of the several Portugália cervejarias around the city—this one enjoys the best location. A limited selection of good, fast food; open until late.
✚ H9 ✉ Cintura do Porto de Lisboa, Armazem 63 ☎ 213 422 138 ⊙ Daily ⊖ Cais do Sodré ⊟ 14, 28, 40, 43

CAFÉS AND PASTELARIAS

ANTIGA CASA DOS PASTÉIS DE BELÉM

This old café and pastry shop in Belém is renowned for its cakes, particularly the distinctive *pastéis de Belém*, tiny flaky tarts filled with custard.

✚ C9 ✉ Rua de Belém 84–8 ☎ 213 637 423 🚌 27, 28, 29, 43, 49, 51; tram 15

CAFÉ A BRASILEIRA

The most famous of Lisbon's venerable coffee-houses at the heart of the fashionable Chiado district was a favored retreat for writers and artists, notably the poet Fernando Pessoa, a statue of whom stands outside on the pavement. Plenty of outdoor tables, and the café remains open until late, when the atmosphere is less sedate.

✚ H8; aIII ✉ Rua Garrett 120 ☎ 213 469 541 🚇 Baixa-Chiado 🚌 58,100; tram 28

CAFÉ CERCA MOURA

Situated close to the Miradouro Santa Luzia in the Largo das Portas do Sol, this café offers fine views of the River Tagus and a good selection of snacks and drinks.

✚ J8; CIII ✉ Largo das Portas do Sol 4 ☎ 218 874 859

CAFÉ MARTINHO DA ARCADA

Like the Nicola (see below) on the Rossio and A Brasileira (see above) in the Chiado, this old coffee-house, founded in 1782, was a haunt of Lisbon's 19th-century literati. The adjoining restaurant is expensive, but the bar is still a good

spot for coffee and snacks. Wood-paneled counter.

✚ J8; bIV ✉ Praça do Comércio 3 ☎ 218 866 213 🚇 Rossio 🚌 11, 13, 81 and all services to Praça do Comércio; tram 15, 18, 25

CAFÉ NICOLA

This lovely old place dating from 1777 was favored by Lisbon's literary set in the 19th century and is now one of the city's most popular cafés—it can be hard to find a table.

✚ H8; aIII ✉ Rua Primeiro de Dezembro; entrance also at Praça Dom Pedro IV 24 (Rossio) ☎ 213 460 579 🚇 Rossio

CASA CHINEZA

Join locals for a mid-morning stand-up snack in this beautifully decorated traditional *pastelaria* in the heart of the Baixa.

✚ J8; bIII ✉ Rua da Aurea 274–78 ☎ 213 423 680 🚇 Baixa-Chiado 🚌 All Avenida da Liberdade services

PASTELARIA BENARD

One of Lisbon's finest and long-established cafés and pastry shops; the desserts are particularly famous. On the Chiado's most fashionable street.

✚ H8; aIII ✉ Rua Garrett 104 ☎ 213 473 133 🚇 Baixa-Chiado

PASTELARIA SUIÇA

This café and pastry shop on Lisbon's main square competes with the Café Nicola (see above) opposite. Both have large and busy terraces.

✚ H8; aIII ✉ Praça Dom Pedro IV 96 ☎ 213 214 095 🚇 Rossio

Pastelarias

If you are looking for a light meal in stylish surroundings, then it is worth considering traditional cafés and pastry shops such as Pastelaria Benard, Café A Brasileira and others (➤ see this page). Though best known as places for coffee and a pastry, they usually serve snacks and sandwiches as well, and may stay open well into the evening.

Drinks

Coffee in Portugal is *café*.

For a small espresso-type shot ask for *um café* or *uma bica*, if you want a dash of milk added ask for *um garoto*. A longer, milkier coffee is *um galão*, but is usually more milk than coffee. For a strong large coffee, ask for a double espresso *(um café duplo)* with milk *(um pouco de leite)*. Tea *(chá)* is very popular, and is served either plain, with milk, *(com leite)* or with lemon *(um chá de limão)*. The most popular yellow beer *(cerveja)* is the Lisbon-brewed Sagres; Sagres Preta is a British-style brown beer. Beer comes in bottles or in measures of a half-liter *(uma caneca)* or quarter-liter in a tall slim glass *(um imperial)*. Mineral water is *água mineral*, either fizzy *(com gás)* or still *(sem gás)*.

SHOPPING DISTRICTS & MALLS

Normal store hours

Traditional shopping in areas such as Baixa, Chiado, Bairro Alto, Avenida da Roma 🕐 8PM–2AM Mon–Fri; Sat 9–1

Shopping malls Colombo, Amoreiras, Vasco da Gama 🕐 Daily 10–midnight

MALLS

AMOREIRAS
Lisbon's first mall is located in the Torres das Amoreiras in the north of the city. This distinctive and very visible building was designed by Tomás Taveira, one of Portugal's leading architects. It contains a hotel, ten movie houses, over 70 cafés and restaurants, and more than 350 stores. Most stay open until late, seven days a week (Sundays are particularly busy).
✚ F7 ✉ Avenida Engenheiro Duarte Pacheco ☎ 213 810 200 🚌 15, 23, 48, 53, 58, 78

COLOMBO
For a postmodern shopping experience join the Lisboetans at the massive Colombo shopping mall located opposite the Benfica football stadium in the north of the city. At the time of completion, this mall claimed to be Iberia's largest with three floors of stores, a hypermarket, restaurants, movies, and a fun park including go-carts and an indoor roller coaster.
✚ D3 ✉ Avenida do Colégio Militar ☎ 217 113 600 Ⓜ Colégio Militar

VASCO DA GAMA
This is Lisbon's newest shopping mall opened in 1999 at the Expo '98 site in the east of the city. It contains all the usual fashion labels, restaurants and a movie complex.
✚ M4 ✉ Avenida Dom João II ☎ 218 930 600 Ⓜ Oriente

DISTRICTS

AVENIDA DA LIBERDADE
Lisbon's main avenue has long been home to many exclusive and stylish clothes stores. This can be a pleasant place to shop while also taking in the beautiful architecture and pavement mosaics. Gift and craft stores are to be found at the Rossio end.
✚ H6–H7 Ⓜ Marquês de Pombal/Avenida/Restauradores 🚌 All Avenida Liberdade services

AVENIDA DE ROMA
Although not as convenient as the purpose built malls, this busy street perhaps offers more variety; as well as major labels there are fashion stores selling shoes, handbags, and clothes.
✚ H3–J4 Ⓜ Roma 🚌 7, 33, and many others

BAIRRO ALTO (► 35)
This district is gaining a reputation as a place to buy clothes, furniture, and household goods.
✚ H8 Ⓜ Baixa-Chiado

BAIXA (► 40)
Many traditional trades still flourish in this area at the heart of the city. In recent years, several fashion chains have opened stores here adding new life to the area.
✚ J8; bIII Ⓜ Baixa-Chiado

CHIADO (► 37)
Chiado is Lisbon's top shopping district, its streets dotted with expensive shoe stores and designer clothes stores.
✚ H8; aIII Ⓜ Baixa-Chiado

FOOD & DRINK

CASA MACÁRIO

Casa Macário in Rua Augusta has bottles of port dating back to 1875 and beyond (at a cost of around 85,000$00). You may not want to spend so much, but port and Madeira are the obvious drinks to take home as a souvenir.

🕂 J4; bIII ✉ Rua Augusta 272–276 ☎ 213 429 029

COISAS DO ARCO DO VINHO

This big wine showroom inside the Centro Cultural de Belém organizes gastronomy sessions and other wine related events, and sells a competently chosen range of wines.

🕂 B10 ✉ Centro Cultural de Belém, Praço do Império ☎ 213 642 031 🚊 Belém (Cascais line from Cais do Sodré) 🚌 27, 28, 29, 43, 49, 51; tram 15

ESPIRITO DO VINHO

This is a wine lovers paradise. It offers the finest wines from Portugal and abroad.

🕂 G8 ✉ Rua Borges Carneiro 38 ☎ 213 859 078 🚌 13, 27

MANUEL TAVARES

For glorious food head for this store in the Baxia, an institution that has been in business for over 100 years.

🕂 J8; bIII ✉ Rua da Betesga 1A/B ☎ 213 424 209 🚊 Rossio

MERCEARIA LIBERDADE

Some of Portugal's best port and Madeira can be found in this charming, typically Portuguese store. They also sell regional handicrafts.

🕂 G7 ✉ Avenida da Liberdade 207 ☎ 213 541 507 🚊 Avenida

O CELEIRO

O Celeiro specializes in natural foods, medicines, vitamins, and cosmetics.

🕂 H8; aIII ✉ Loja 1, Rua 1 de Dezembro 65 ☎ 213 422 463 🚊 Rossio

PANIFICAÇÃO MECÂNICA

There are many excellent bakeries around town, but if you happen to be in the area of Campo de Ourique, this store offers a huge selection of bread, cakes, and pastries.

🕂 G8 ✉ Rua Silva Carvalho, 209–223 🚊 Rato 🚌 58, 74

MARKETS

Lisbon's main flea market takes place in Campo de Santa Clara (▶ 46 🕒 Tue AM; Sat all day). Larger and extremely colorful food markets are held around the Cais do Sodré railroad station (🕒 Mon–Sat 6–2). The Bairro Alto neighborhood market is in Rua da Atalaia (🕒 Mon–Sat 7–2).

WINE SHOPS

Try: Co-operative Wine Shop in the Chiado.

🕂 H8; aIII; IV ✉ Rua do Alecrim 24, Chiado ☎ 213 423 590

Napoleão in the Baixa.

🕂 J8; bIII ✉ Rua dos Fanqueiros 70 ☎ 218 872 042

Ulitro in the Bairro Alto.

🕂 H8; aIII ✉ Rua da Barroca ☎ 213 425 213

Vintage

Vintage port—the best port—is made from the grapes of one year only, and then only if that year's harvest has been specially declared of vintage quality. It is bottled after two to four years in the cask and then ages for at least ten years in the bottle. Since 1974, a port must have been bottled in Portugal to be labeled a vintage. Late-bottled port (LBV) is a port that is not quite up to vintage standard, but is still deemed good enough to mature in the bottle rather than the cask. Typically it is bottled after about four to six years. Crucially, port which ages in the bottle matures by reduction, turning a deep-red color. Port that ages in the cask matures through oxidation, and turns towards an amber color. The longer in the cask, the lighter the color.

FASHION, LEATHER & FOOTWEAR

Fashion capital

Fashion designers are a relatively recent phenomenon in Lisbon (since the mid-1980s), but now with the help of such fashion events as the yearly *Moda Lisboa*, usually held in April, and *Vestir o Milenio* (Dressing the Millennium) in June, national designers are getting the publicity they deserve. From established names such as Fátima Lopes and Ana Salazar to the more recent talent of Maria Gambina and José António Tenente, Portuguese creations can now be found in stores and on the catwalks of Paris, London, and Barcelona.

ANA SALAZAR

Ana Salazar is perhaps the best-known Portuguese fashion designer on the international stage. She is known primarily for her daring designs and for special stretch fabrics. Currently, she has two outlets in the city. The most central is the store on Rua do Carmo, in the Chiado.

H8; a–bIII ✉ Rua do Carmo 87 ☎ 213 472 289 Ⓜ Rossio 🚌 2, 31, 36, 41;
H3–J4 ✉ Avenida de Roma 16e ☎ 218 486 799 Ⓜ Roma

CASA DO TURISTA

This store does sell a selection of tacky souvenirs, but it also has some tasteful regional clothing and accessories including sweaters from Póvoa do Varzim near Oporto and scarves from the Minho.

H7; all ✉ Avenida da Liberdade 159 ☎ 212 973 193 Ⓜ Rossio/Avenida

COELHO PELEIRO

Excellent for leather belts and can make leather backed fabric belts to order from your own material in its workshop next door. It also sells a variety of accessories.

J8; bIII ✉ Rua da Conceição 85 ☎ 213 425 770 Ⓜ Baixa-Chiado

ELDORADO

Secondhand vintage clothing, mainly from the 1950s, 60s, and 70s. It also sells records.

H8; alll ✉ Rua do Norte 23 ☎ 213 423 935 Ⓜ Baixa-Chiado

FÁTIMA LOPES

A degree of daring would be required in order to wear Fátima Lopes' creations, but this designer has become a favorite on the Portuguese catwalks. Another branch can be found on the Avenida de Roma.

H8; alll ✉ Rua da Atalaia 36 ☎ 213 225 865 Ⓜ Baixa-Chiado 🚌 58, 100; tram 28

GALEÃO

In the heart of the Baixa, Galeão has a fine collection of leather belts and luggage.

J8; bIII ✉ Rua Augusta 190 ☎ 213 470 886 Ⓜ Baixa-Chiado

JOSÉ ANTÓNIO TENENTE

José António Tenente opened his store on Rua do Carmo in 1990. Lines are considered more conservative than other Barrio Alto boutiques.

H8; alll ✉ Travessa do Carmo 8 ☎ 213 422 560 Ⓜ Baixa-Chiado

LUVARIA ULISSES

This tiny store is a treasure trove of gloves in every material imaginable, including silk, satin, lace, leather, and cotton.

H8; alll ✉ Rua do Carmo 87–A ☎ 213 420 295 Ⓜ Rossio

SAPATEIRO LISBOENSE

This store is just one of the many in the Baixa selling quality shoes, bags, suitcases, and belts.

J8; bIII ✉ Rua Augusta 202–204 ☎ 213 426 712 Ⓜ Baixa-Chiado

ART, MAPS, BOOKS & MUSIC

BRITÂNICA
If you find you need more reading material while in Lisbon, this bookstore in the Rato specializes in books in the English language.
✚ H7 ✉ Rua de São Marçal 8
☎ 213 428 472 ▣ 58

FNAC
One of the many foreign retail chains to open in Lisbon over the past few years, FNAC offers the most comprehensive selection of books (including foreign language sections), music, and maps.
✚ D3 ✉ Shop No. A–103, Colombo Shopping Mall ☎ 217 114 237 ⊜ Colégio Militar;
✚ H8; bIII ✉ Rua Nova do Almada 104–110 ☎ 213 221 800 ⊜ Baixa-Chiado

GALLERIA 111
By far the most famous commercial art gallery in Lisbon, the outlying Galleria 111 has been in business since 1964. It shows and sells only the very best and most expensive of Portuguese artists, and so is for serious buyers and browsers only. Art enthusiasts who are not well-heeled might invest in its postcards, art books, and cheaper prints, drawings and etchings.
✚ H4 ✉ Campo Grande 111–113 ☎ 217 977 418 ⊜ Entrecampos ▣ 36a, 47

GALERIA SESIMBRA
Situated near the Ritz Hotel, this gallery displays the finest of Portuguese painting, sculpture, and ceramics along with several foreign artists now resident in Portugal. It is best known for its hand-made Agulha tapestries.
✚ G6 ✉ Rua do Castilho
☎ 213 870 291 ⊜ Marquês de Pombal

LIVRARIA BUCHHOLZ
This pleasantly jumbled three-floor store not only sells a range of English-language books (as well as an excellent range of Portuguese titles), but also is one of the few outlets to sell Portuguese folk and other ethnic music.
✚ H7 ✉ Rua Duque de Palmela 4 ☎ 213 170 580 ⊜ Marquês de Pombal

TABACARIA MÓNACO
This tiny newspaper seller and tobacconist (*tabacaria*) is a Lisbon landmark. Founded in 1893, it preserves a wonderful art nouveau ambience, with a lovely tiled and painted interior. On a practical level, it is a good place to come for maps, guides, and foreign newspapers and magazines.
✚ H8–J8; bII–bIII ✉ Praça Dom Pedro IV 21 (Rossio) ☎ 213 468 191 ⊙ Daily 9–7:30 ⊜ Rossio ▣ 1, 2, 11 and all other services to the Rossio ❓ No credit cards

VALENTIM DE CARVALHO
Fado is not to all tastes, but if you want an authentic souvenir of your visit to Lisbon this is the place. Also contemporary Portuguese pop and rock.
✚ H8–J8; bII–bIII ✉ Praça Dom Pedro IV 59 (Rossio) ☎ 213 224 400 ⊜ Rossio ▣ 1, 2, 11 and all other services to the Rossio

Lisbon's Poet
Luís de Camões, adventurous, passionate, and a lover of the fast life, was born to minor nobility in 1524. Well educated but penniless, he was banished from court after an unsavory love affair and brawl, becoming instead a soldier on active duty in Ceuta (1547). Two years later he returned to Lisbon, but another brawl led to 9 months in prison. Early release was granted on the condition he join the King's service in India. Storms and shipwrecks marked his journey, notably one in the Mekong Delta when he had to swim to rescue his manuscript of *Os Lusíadas* (The Lusiads). This, his major work, was much influenced by his journey and was published on his return to Lisbon in 1572. It was not until Spain's Philip II (reigning as king of Portugal) praised his work that it became recognized as a symbol of Portuguese nationalism. *Os Lusíadas* is available in all good bookstores and translations in English are also available.

CRAFTS, GIFTS & SOUVENIRS

Barcelos Cocks

Although originally from Barcelos in the north, it's hard to avoid the ubiquitous "Barcelos Cock" painted pottery and wooden models that assault you from every souvenier store and stall, especially since adapted by the tourist authority as their emblem. The cock's story is simple and reports a tale told across the Iberian peninsula. A pilgrim heading for Santiago de Compostela was unjustly accused of theft on leaving Barcelos. Despite pleading innocence he was found guilty and sentenced to death. Looking at the roast cockerel served for the judges dinner, he invoked the help of St. James, saying that if he were innocent the dead cock would crow. This it promptly did and the man was released.

ARTESANATO REGIONAL PORTUGUÊS

One of the oldest handicraft stores in Lisbon (opened 1960s) with a wide assortment of genuine handmade articles displayed in 300 yards of showrooms a block down from the Post Office building.

H7; all ⊠ Praça dos Restauradores 64 ☎ 213 477 875 Ⓜ Restauradores

CASA ALVES

Selling items worked in copper including shallow round-bottomed copper dishes known as *cataplanas*, in which the rich fish and seafood dish from which it takes its name is served.

J8; bIII ⊠ Rua Augusta 51 ☎ 213 475 429 Ⓜ Baixa-Chiado

CASA DAS CORTIÇAS

Cork (*cortiças*) is one of Portugal's most distinctive exports—it controls a vast proportion of the world's trade in the commodity. This singular little store sells all sorts of objects—many rather unlikely—fashioned from the material, providing a uniquely Portuguese gift or souvenir to take home.

G7–H7 ⊠ Rua da Escola Politécnica 4–6 ☎ 213 425 858 🚍 58

CASA DE BORDADOS DE MADEIRA

Situated inside the Avenida Palace hotel, this store sells embroideries from Viana do Castelo and Madeira (expensive) and the famous fishermen's sweaters from Póvoa do Varzim.

H8; alll ⊠ Rua 1 de Dezembro 135–139 ☎ 213 421 447 Ⓜ Restauradores 🚍 1, 2, 36, 44 or any of Avenida de Liberdade services

CASA MACIEL

Lisbon is full of long-established stores: this one was founded in 1810, and has grown from a small metal-working factory into an award-winning outlet for all manner of beautifully crafted work in metal. Pieces can be made to individual designs if required.

H8; all–alll ⊠ Rua da Misericórdia 63–5 ☎ 213 422 451 Ⓜ Rossio 🚍 58, 100; tram 28

CUSTÓDIO CARDOSO PEREIRA

Store selling the beautiful 12-stringed guitars used to accompany the fado singers.

H8; alll ⊠ Largo do Chiado 20 ☎ 213 224 180 Ⓜ Baixa-Chiado

FÁBRICA DE CÉRAMICA VIÚVA LAMEGO

Not as venerable as the Fábrica Sant'Anna (see below), this factory nonetheless dates back to 1879. The factory store is adorned with tiles on its exterior, and sells mainly copies of traditional designs, together with a small selection of pottery. It will also design and make tiles to order.

J7; bl ⊠ Largo do Intendente Pina Manique 25 ☎ 218 852 408 Ⓜ Intendente 🚍 7, 8, 40; tram 17, 28

FÁBRICA SANT'ANNA

This historic company has been Portugal's leading producer of *azulejos*, or decorated tiles, since 1741. The Rua do Alecrim address is the store for its beautifully decorated products, many of which are based on traditional designs. It is also possible to visit the main factory by prior arrangement.

⊞ H8 ✉ Rua do Alecrim 95–7 ☎ 213 422 537 🚍 58, 100; tram 28. Factory ⊞ D9 ✉ Calçada da Boa Hora 96 ☎ 213 638 292

JOALHARIA DO CARMO

In business for almost a century, Joalharia do Carmo has few rivals when it comes to gold and silver filigree jewelry. It offers a wide variety of products, virtually all of them handmade.

⊞ H8; alll–blll ✉ Rua do Carmo 87b ☎ 213 424 200 🚇 Rossio 🚍 21, 31, 36, 41, all services to Rossio

KÁ

Selling modern pieces by up-and-coming artists in papier-mâché, glass, metal, stone, and wood. In the Centro Cultural de Belém complex.

⊞ B10 ✉ Centro Cultural de Belém, Praça do Império ☎ 213 612 400 🚇 Belém (Cascais line from Cais do Sodré) 🚍 27, 28, 29, 43, 49, 51; tram 15

PAÍS EM LISBOA

Hidden in the narrow streets of the Bairro Alto, this store specializes in dolls dressed in traditional costume. It also has a fine selection of linen.

⊞ H8 ✉ Rua de Teixeira 25 🚇 Restauradores–Elevadar da Gloria 🚍 58

SANTOS OFICIOS

This handicraft store founded in 1995 is housed inside a restored 18th-century stable. It sells handmade products from around the country including ceramics, linens, and sheepskin slippers.

⊞ J8; blll ✉ Rua da Madalena 87 ☎ 218 872 031 🚇 Baixa-Chiado 🚍 7, 40; trams 15

SARMENTO

The family-run firm of Sarmento has been Lisbon's most prestigious jeweler for almost a hundred years. The gold, silverware, and filigree here are some of the most exquisite in Portugal.

⊞ H8; blll ✉ Rua Aurea (Rua do Ouro) 251 ☎ 213 426 774 🚇 Baixa-Chiado 🚍 Tram 28

TABACARIA A PHOENIX LTD

Found in the Rossio, this *tabacaria* (tobacconists) does a line in regional baskets, which can make ideal gifts. It also sells guide books, lighters, and other gift items.

⊞ H8; blll ✉ Praça Dom Pedro IV 40 ☎ 213 225 769 🚇 Rossio 🚍 14, 37, 43, 59 or any other Rossio service

VIÚVA LAMEGO

This is one of the top stores in Lisbon for beautiful tiles, including faïence and copies of traditional designs. Order you own design.

⊞ H8; alll ✉ Calçada do Sacramento 29 ☎ 213 469 692 🚇 Baixa-Chiado

Casa Batalha

At the time of the great Chiado fire (1988), Casa Batalha had already been serving its customers on Rua Nova do Almada for 350 years. The tradition of selling costume jewelry and accessories has been passed down through seven generations since 1635. It is now back trading in the heart of Lisbon at its age old location.

✉ Rua Nova do Almada, 75–77 🚇 Baixa-Chiado

Tiles galore

Azulejos have been decorating not only palaces, churches, chapels, and public buildings for centuries but also the homes of Portugal, helping to waterproof against the winter rains. Very popular as souvenirs, you can find a vast array of fine hand-painted, antique, and contemporary tiles to give to your friends or adorn your home.

FOR THE HOME

Arraiolos carpets

The attractive little town of Arraiolos lies 90 miles east of Lisbon and has been famous for centuries for its superlative hand-woven carpets. The patterns originally owed much to Moorish and Persian designs, but these days, while still beautiful, they tend to be less complex. Prices are fairly high whether buying one in Lisbon or Arraiolos.

ARQUITECTÓNICA

This is a good place to go if looking for avant-garde designer furniture and furnishings.

⊞ H7 ✉ Rua da Escola Politécnica 94 ☎ 213 906 721 🚇 Rato 🚌 58, 100

A TRINIDADE

As well as having a fine collection of antique porcelain and religious art, this antique store on the Rua do Alecrim specilizes in antique furniture.

⊞ H8; alll ✉ Rua do Alecrim 79–81 ☎ 213 424 660 🚇 Baixa-Chiado 🚌 58, 100

CASA DAS VELAS DO LORETO

This venerable store in the Bairro Alto has been in the business of producing candles of all shapes and sizes for over 200 years.

⊞ H8; alll ✉ Rua do Loreto 53 ☎ 213 425 387 🚇 Restauradores

CASA QUINTÃO

Some of Portugal's most beautiful and expensive handicrafts are the sensational carpets made in and around the Alentejan town of Arraiolos (see panel). This Chiado store is one of Lisbon's principal outlets for the carpets, which are priced by area and according to the density of the stitching.

⊞ H8; alll ✉ Rua Serpa Pinto 12A ☎ 213 465 837 🚌 58, 100; tram 28

CASA REGIONAL DA ILHA VERDE

Selling all manner of artifacts from the Ilha Verde (Green Island),

more commonly known as San Miguel in the Azores. Fabrics, linens, and embroidery are specialties. Much of the work is based on age-old designs.

⊞ H7 ✉ Rua de Paiva de Andrade 4 ☎ 213 425 974 🚇 Restauradores 🚌 1, 2, 36, 44 and Avenida do Liberdade services

DEPOSITO DA MARINHA GRANDE

These no-nonsense Bairro Alto stores are outlets for Marinha Grande's own reasonably priced glass and china, many based on old, unusual designs. The firm is long established, and its Atlantis glass is particularly well known in Portugal.

⊞ G7–G8 ✉ Rua de São Bento 234–242 ☎ 213 963 234 🚇 Rato 🚌 6 49;
⊞ G7–G8 ✉ Rua de São Bento 418–420 ☎ 213 963 096 🚇 Rato 🚌 6, 49

MADEIRA HOUSE

Specializes in high quality cottons, linens, and gift items from the island of Madeira. It has two outlets, one in the Baixa and the other on the Avenida da Liberdade.

⊞ J8; bIII ✉ Rua Augusta 131–135 ☎ 213 426 813 🚇 Rossio/Baixa-Chiado 🚌 All services to Praça do Comécio or Rossio

M. MURTEIRA

If walking up to the Castelo de São Jorge, you will probably pass this charming antiques store selling curiosities from the 18–19th century. You may find anything from bed heads to bird cages.

➕ J8; clll ✉ Rua Augusto Rosa
19–21 ☎ 218 863 851
🚌 37; tram 28

OLARIA DO DESTERRO

Just off the Rua da Palma
Almirante Reis is this 150-
year-old store selling
traditional earthenware
pieces such as plates and
casseroles.
➕ J7; bl ✉ Rua Nova do
Desterro 14 ☎ 218 850 013
🚇 Martim Moniz/Intendente
🚌 7, 8, 40; tram 17, 28

PRÍNCIPE REAL

This prestigious firm
produces and sells some of
the loveliest table linens,
cottons, and other fabrics
imaginable. Royalty and
all manner of rich and
famous clients have
patronized the store over
the years. Sheets and
tablecloths are good buys,
and prices are not as
outrageous as you might
expect.
➕ G7–H7 ✉ Rua da Escola
Politécnica 12–14 ☎ 213 431
455 🚌 58, 100

RETROSARIA E ESTABLECIMENTOS NARDO

If looking for anything
related to haberdashery,
try this store in the Baixa
which offers a wide
selection of buttons,
ribbons, cords, and
threads.
➕ J8; blll ✉ Rua da Conceição
62–64 ☎ 213 421 350
🚇 Baixa-Chiado

SOLAR

Rua Dom Pedro V is
home to several of the
cities best antique stores.
This particular one is good

for original tiles taken
from manor houses and
historic buildings dating
back to the 15th century.
It also has a good selection
of pewter ware and
furniture.
➕ H7 ✉ Rua Dom Pedro V
68–70 ☎ 213 465 522
🚇 Restauradores 🚌 58,100

TERESA ALECRIM

This store is named after
its owner who produces
fine high quality
embroideries created in
plain or patterned cotton
in the Laura Ashley style.
Pillowcases, sheets,
towels, and covers are but
a few items she offers.
➕ H8; blll ✉ Rua Nova do
Almada 76 ☎ 213 421 831
🚇 Baixa-Chiado 🚌 2; tram 28
Also at ✉ Amoreiras Complex,
Shop No.1116 ✉ Avenida da
Roma 68

VISTA ALEGRE

In business since 1824,
this prestigious firm is
renowned in Portugal
and beyond for its
exquisite porcelain
dinner sets and china. It
supplied Portuguese
royalty until 1910, and
today still supplies china
to many of the royal
families of Europe. It
also sells less expensive
but nonetheless coveted
tableware for everyday
use from some half-a-
dozen outlets around
the city, including:
➕ H8; alll ✉ Largo do Chiado
18 ☎ 213 475 489 🚌 28;
✉ Rua Castilho 39 – 5°;
✉ Avenida da Igreja 4f;
✉ Amoreiras Complex Shop No.
2028;
✉ Colombo Complex Shop No.
1053

Decorséculo

One of the Bairro Alto's most
interesting stores is Decorséculo in
Rua do Século, offering one-off
pieces of original designer
furniture and household objects.
➕ H7, H8 ✉ Rua do Século
68 ☎ 213 431 153
🚌 tram 28

Antiques in Lisbon

Whether you are looking for
genuine antiques or just bric-a-
brac, you will find it in the stores
around Rua de São Bento, Rua
Dom Pedro, Rua do Alecrim, and
around the Castelo São Jorge.
Aritfacts range from religious
carvings to dolls, together with an
array of furniture and items for
the home.

BARS & NIGHTCLUBS

Solar do Vinho do Porto

Owned by the Port Wine Institute, the Solar do Vinho do Porto is a large, relaxed, and rather refined bar given over entirely to port. It is one of the places in Lisbon that you should visit at least once. You can order by the glass or bottle from a *lista de vinhos*, which includes over 300 red and white ports. It is located in a fine old townhouse in the Bairro Alto, close to the upper station of the Elevador da Glória.

✚ H7 ✉ Rua de São Pedro de Alcântara 45 R/C ☎ 213 475 707 🕔 8PM–3AM 🚌 58, 100

How much?

In theory, in most top Lisbon clubs there is no official charge at the door but drinks carry a surcharge once inside. In practice, women are rarely asked to pay at the door while the fate of their male companions depends on the mood of the doorman. Some may demand up to 5,000$00.

ALCÂNTARA CAFÉ

This designer bar is among the smartest and trendiest in Lisbon. After eating in the excellent restaurant, cross the little interior bridge to the adjoining, stylish Alcântara-Mar nightclub.

✉ Rua da Cozinha Económica ☎ 213 636 432 🕔 8PM–4AM; nightclub open Thu–Sat 🚋 Alcântara (Cascais line) 🚌 12, 20, 22, 28; tram 15

BACHUS

As well as a top restaurant, Bachus offers one of the city's most refined bars. Oriental carpets, fine furniture, and intimate lighting make this a favorite among Lisbon's glamorous.

✚ H8; alll ✉ Largo da Trinidade 8–9 ☎ 213 422 828 🕔 Mon–Fri 12PM–2AM 🚋 Baixa-Chiado 🚌 58, 100

CHAPITÔ

A very relaxed and enjoyable outdoor bar by the castle, with good food, an attractive setting, and gorgeous views.

✚ J8; clll ✉ Rua Costa do Castelo 1–7 ☎ 218 881 834 🕔 Mon–Sat 🚌 37; tram 12, 28

FRÁGIL

Opened in 1983, this is one of the oldest, most popular and self-consciously trendy of the Bairro's many club-bars.

✚ H8; alll ✉ Rua da Atalaia 128 ☎ 213 469 578 🕔 Mon–Sat 🚌 58, 100; tram 28

KAPITAL

So trendy that you have to pass a style test at the door before you can get in.

With three floors of music and bars, plus an excellent rooftop terrace.

✚ G8 ✉ Avenida 24 de Julho 68 ☎ 213 957 101 🕔 Tue–Sat to 5:30AM; Sun–Mon to 4AM 🚋 Santos 🚌 14, 28, 32, 40, 43; tram 15, 18

KREMLIN

Almost as hip as Kapital (see above), and almost as difficult to get into, so dress in full clubbing mode. Gets going after about 2AM and closes around 7AM.

✚ G8 ✉ Escadinhas da Praia 5 ☎ 213 908 768 🕔 Tue; Thu–Sat 🚋 Santos 🚌 14, 28, 32, 40, 43; tram 15, 18

PLATEAU

If you have no joy at Kremlin (see above), or want something a little less trendy and with more mainstream rock and pop.

✚ G8 ✉ Escadinhas da Praia 7 ☎ 213 965 116 🕔 Tue–Sat 🚋 Santos 🚌 14, 28, 40, 43; tram 15, 18

PAVILHÃO CHINÊS

Covered with a jumble of fans, china, sheet music, and other miscellaneous *objets d'art*, the drinks and cocktails here are reasonably priced.

✚ H7 ✉ Rua Dom Pedro V 89 ☎ 213 424 729 🕔 Mon–Sat 6PM–2AM; Sun 9PM–2AM 🚋 Restauradores 🚌 58, 100

SNOB

Quieter, classier Bairro Alto bar with wooden booths, leather seats, and soothing green baize.

✚ H8; alll ✉ Rua da Atalaia-Rua do Século 178 ☎ 213 463 723 🕔 8PM–2AM 🚌 58, 100; tram 28

LIVE MUSIC

ANOS 60

If you want to relive the 1960s, this bar, which also serves light snacks, plays live music daily. Intimate and friendly.

🔢 J7; bll–dl ✉ Largo do Terreirinho 21 ☎ 218 873 444 🕐 Tue–Sat 9:30–4AM 🚇 Martim Moniz

HOT CLUBE DE PORTUGAL

This little basement club has long enjoyed a reputation as Lisbon's best place for jazz. Portuguese and visiting performers.

🔢 H7; all ✉ Praça de Alegria 39, off Avenida da Liberdade ☎ 213 467 369 🕐 Tue–Wed for jam sessions, Thu–Sat for concerts: two sessions 11PM and 12:30AM 🚇 Avenida

PAVILHÃO ATLANTICO & PRAÇA SONY

Situated out to the east of the city at the Expo '98 site, both of these venues offer regular live music shows and concerts. Contact the tourist office for information or any of the cities main music stores.

🔢 M1 ✉ Parque das Nações, Pavilhão do Atlantico ☎ 21 881 0900 🔢 M12 ✉ Praça Sony ☎ 218 918 409 🕐 Thu–Sat 10PM–2AM 🚇 Oriente

PÉ SUJO

This small club, hidden away in the Alfama district, offers live Brazilian samba, forró, and batucada daily.

🔢 J8; clll ✉ Largo de Sâo Martinho 6–7 ☎ 218 866 144

PILLON

Danny Silva, this club's resident artist provides Cape Verdian music daily. Tuesday nights are apparently their most "happening."

🔢 E8 ✉ Rua do Alvito, 10 ☎ 213 636 265 🕐 Daily 10–4AM 🚌 12, 42, 51

RITZ CLUB

A big and buzzy African club just off Avenida da Liberdade. Excellent African music from a resident band or visiting stars.

🔢 H7; all ✉ Rua da Glória 57 ☎ 213 425 140 🕐 Mon–Sat 🚇 Restauradores/Avenida 🚌 1, 2, 9, 11, 31 and all other Avenida da Liberdade services

ROCK CITY

A little nearer the center of town than most of the riverfront nightspots, this large club not only offers live rock/pop music but also has a restaurant, gardens, and terrace with great views over the river. It attracts a fairly young crowd.

🔢 G9 ✉ Rua Cintrura do Porto de Lisboa, Store 225 ☎ 213 428 640 🕐 Tue–Sun 🚇 Cais do Sodré 🚌 14, 28, 32, 40, 43; tram 15, 18

SALSA LATINA

Conveniently situated near the many restaurants and bars at the Doca de Santo Amaro, this fairly recent addition (1999) to the Lisbon scene offers the cities best Latin sounds, livened up at the weekends by a live Cuban band.

🔢 E9 ✉ Antiga Gare Marítima de Alcântara ☎ 213 950 550 🕐 12–4AM 🚇 Alcântara (Cascais line) 🚌 28

Places

For years you had to go no further than the streets of the Bairro Alto to find a good night out. These days bars and clubs are increasingly further afield, because of official urban regeneration policies and attempts to take noisy late-night entertainment away from the residential Bairro. Trendy new places have opened on and around the Avenida da 24 de Julho (along the waterfront west of Cais do Sodré), the Alcântara district (notably the fast-growing and increasingly fashionable Doca do Santo Amaro, also on the waterfront), and to a lesser extent the fringes of the Alfama and Graça districts east of the city center. Gay bars and clubs cluster largely in the Rato, on the fringes of the Bairro Alto.

MOVIES & PERFORMING ARTS

Tickets and information

You can obtain information and tickets for a wide variety of concerts, films, plays, and shows by calling in person at the Agência de Bilhetes para Espectáculos Públicos (ABEP), on the corner of Praça dos Restauradores (☎ 213 475 824). The tourist office in the same square offers the *Agenda Cultural*, a free monthly listings magazine. The Museu Calouste Gulbenkian issues details of its own program of events. The local *Diário de Notícias* and *O Independente* newspapers carry listings (in Portuguese) and the Friday editions carry free pull-out listings supplements. The Centro Cultural de Belém issues monthly listings booklets for its own events.

MOVIES

Movie-going is a pleasure in Lisbon. Unlike those in many European cities, Lisbon movie houses usually show movies in their original language, with Portuguese subtitles. This means that English-speaking visitors can enjoy mainstream Hollywood releases without dubbing. As a bonus, some houses are old-fashioned places, and still have their original art nouveau and art deco interiors. The most popular movie houses among the Lisboetans tend to be the complexes in the major shopping malls as they are the newest and offer the best sound and quality (► 70).
Tickets, already low-priced by most visitors' standards, are even more inexpensive on Mondays, but be early to get a seat.

ART-HOUSE

Classic films, re-runs and avant-garde movies are shown at a variety of art-houses, most notably the national film theater:
Instituto da Cinemateca Portuguesa ✚ H7 ✉ Rua Barata Salgueiro 39 ☎ 213 596 262 🕐 Programs twice daily 🚇 Avenida

MAINSTREAM

The majority of big, first-release movies are shown in movie houses clustered around Praça dos Restauradores and off the Avenida da Liberdade. Major first-run movie houses include:

Coliseu ✚ H7; all ✉ Rua Portas de Santo Antão ☎ 213 240 580 🚇 Restauradores
São Jorge ✚ H7; all ✉ Avenida da Liberdade 175 ☎ 213 579 144 🚇 Restauradores
Tivoli ✚ H7; all ✉ Avenida da Liberdade 188 ☎ 213 198 900 🚇 Restauradores

CLASSICAL MUSIC

The main driving force behind classical music in Lisbon (and many other cultural activities) is the Fundação Calouste Gulbenkian (Calouste Gulbenkian Foundation). It sponsors its own choir, orchestra, and ballet company, and its complex of buildings north of the Parque Eduardo VII boasts three major concert halls and facilities for outdoor performances. During the October to June season, the Foundation presents a wide range of classical and jazz concerts, from small-scale chamber recitals to programs requiring full symphony orchestras. At other times of the year, the Foundation is responsible for all manner of musical and other events around the city. Details of its program can be obtained from the Gulbenkian Museum (► 33), which is housed in the Foundation complex, or from the tourist office and newspaper listings.
Fundação Calouste Gulbenkian ✚ G5 ✉ Avenida de Berna 45 ☎ 217 823 000 🚇 São Sebastião/Praça de Espanha 🚌 16, 26, 31, 46, 56

OTHER CONCERT VENUES

A full range of classical music performances is held in the Teatro Nacional de São Carlos and Teatro Municipal de São Luís. Recitals are also given in the two auditoria in the Centro Cultural de Belém out in the western suburb of Belém.

Teatro Nacional de São Carlos ✚ H8; aIII–aIV ✉ Rua Serpa Pinto 9 ☎ 213 465 914 🕔 Box office: daily 1–7 🚇 Baixo-Chiado 🚌 100, 58; tram 28

Teatro Municipal de São Luís ✚ aIII–aIV ✉ Rua António Maria Cardoso 40 ☎ 213 427 172 🚇 Baixa-Chiado 🚌 58, 100; tram 28

Centro Cultural de Belém ✚ B10 ✉ Praça do Império ☎ 213 612 444 🚉 Belém (Cascais line from Cais do Sodré) 🚌 29, 43; tram 15

In summer, concerts are held throughout the city (many of them free), particularly in churches, including:
Sé (the cathedral, ► 42)
São Roque (► 36)
Basílica da Estrela (► 32)
São Vicente de Fora (► 55)
The ruined Convento do Carmo, now the Museu Arqueológico do Carmo (► 38)
Igreja dos Mártires, Rua Garrett in the Chiado.

OPERA AND BALLET

Lisbon's principal opera and ballet performances take place in the beautiful 18th-century Teatro Nacional de São Carlos and the adjacent Teatro Municipal de São Luís in the Bairro Alto. Note that neither the opera nor the ballet season extends right through the summer: typically the seasons run from mid-September to July. The Calouste Gulbenkian Foundation has its own ballet company and facilities for indoor and outdoor performances. Opera and ballet sometimes are among events held at the Centro Cultural de Belém (see above).

THEATER

The performing arts in Lisbon are enjoying more popularity than ever with young people involved both as spectators and performers. Most of Lisbon's theater performances are in Portuguese. However, you can sample the traditional musical revues without a grasp of the language. Small theaters are dotted across the city; the main performance space is the Rossio's eye-catching Teatro Nacional de Dona Maria II, completed in 1846. Many performances are in the Coliseu complex.

Teatro Nacional Dona Maria ✚ H8; a, bII ✉ Praça Dom Pedro IV (Rossio) ☎ 213 422 210 🚇 Rossio 🚌 1, 2, 31, 36, 41 and all Rossio services

Coliseu ✚ H7; aII ✉ Rua Portas de Santo Antão ☎ 213 240 580 🚇 Restauradores

Sintra music festival

Each year in June and July, a series of concerts, ballet performances, and other events are held in palaces and country houses in and around Sintra. Venues include the Palácio Nacional in Sintra (► 20), the gorgeous pink palace of Queluz, and the palace at Seteias, now a luxury hotel (► 84). Details from the tourist information office in Lisbon (► 90) or Sintra (► 20).

FADO

Cover charge

Fado houses don't charge admission, but nearly all make a cover charge. This usually buys you a couple of drinks. Performances usually start around 9PM, the real action may begin to hot up only between 11PM and midnight. The price guides for restaurants shown on this page indicate the cost of a meal (➤ 62).

History of fado

Lisbon and Coimbra are the two great centers of fado—a melancholy form of traditional singing accompanied by guitar. Passion, fate, and regrets are the main themes. It may originate from African slave songs, or have Moorish roots. In Lisbon, the singer (*fadista*) is nearly always a woman, and is accompanied by one or two impassive male guitarists. Coimbra fado is sung by men, and has a less heartrending quality.

The real thing

Sadly, as with many traditional forms of culture, some old clubs have been smartened up and the music stripped of its soul for the benefit of tourists. Try to steer clear of places that have uniformed staff on the door and where photographers hustle to sell you pictures of you taken at your table.

ADEGA DO MACHADO ($$)

Once one of the oldest and among the most revered of all the fado clubs in Portugal, where now you can exexperience fado and folk dancing in traditional costume, albeit rather touristy.

H8; alll ⊠ Rua do Norte 91 ☎ 213 428 713 🕐 Tue–Sun 8PM–3AM 🚇 Baixa-Chiado 🚌 58, 100; tram 28

ADEGA DO RIBATEJO ($$)

Popular with locals, there are fado performances by paid singers and also by the cooks or the management.

H8; alll ⊠ Rua Diário de Notícias 23 ☎ 213 468 343 🕐 Mon–Sat 8PM–2AM 🚇 Baixi-Chiado 🚌 58, 100; tram 28

A SEVERA ($$$)

Named after a legendary 19th-century gypsy *fadista*, it attracts many of the big names in the fado firmament and charges high prices.

H8; alll ⊠ Rua das Gáveas 51 ☎ 213 464 006 🕐 Fri–Wed 8PM–3 🚇 Baixi-Chiado 🚌 58, 100; tram 28

LISBOA A NOITE ($$$)

One of the more touristy of the city's fado houses. It is fine if you want to eat and listen in comfortable surroundings, but not if you want the rough-edged authenticity of a genuine dancing club and real fado.

H8; alll ⊠ Rua das Gáveas 69 ☎ 213 468 557 🕐 Mon–Sat 8PM–3 🚇 Baixi-Chiado 🚌 58, 100; tram 28 ❓ Performances start at 9:30PM

O SENHOR VINHO ($$$)

Located in Lapa, this celebrated club is some way to the west of the tourist haunts of the Alfama and Bairro Alto. As a result it is far more authentic—though not necessarily much more inexpensive—than many other clubs.

G8 ⊠ Rua do Meio à Lapa 18 ☎ 213 972 681 🕐 Mon–Sat 8:30PM–2:30AM 🚌 13, 27; tram 25, 28

PARREIRINHA DA ALFAMA ($$)

Another of the city's more venerable clubs featuring some of the century's greatest names in fado. However, both cover charge and food prices are lower than those of its big-name rivals. No dancing.

J8; clll ⊠ Beco do Espírito Santo 1, off Largo do Chafariz de Dentro ☎ 218 868 209 🕐 Mon–Sat 8–2AM 🚌 37; tram 28

RESTAURANTE SÃO CAETANO ($$)

Worth visiting for the food as well as the fado, with an non-touristy atmosphere.

F8 ⊠ Rua de São Caetano à Lapa 27 ☎ 213 974 792 🕐 Mon–Fri lunch, dinner; Sat, Sun dinner only 🚌 13, 27; tram 25

TIMPANAS ($$)

The show in this fado house in the Alcântara district is organized with dinner and folk dancing rather than spontaneous fado, but there's still some good singing.

F9 ⊠ Rua G Rola ☎ 213 906 655 🚇 Alcântara Mar 🚌 27, 40, 49, 60; tram 15, 18

SPORTS & LEISURE

BULLFIGHTS

Bullfighting is every bit as popular in Portugal as in Spain, and though less gory than in Spain as the Portuguese concentrate on fine horsemanship, it also involves taunting and weakening the bull by spearing it with *banderilhas* (lances decorated with ribbons) and then killing it (but not in the ring). The spectacle is not for everyone. Bullfights take place on various dates between Easter and September at Portugal's largest ring, the Praça de Touros do Campo Pequeno. Call for details.
🚇 H4 ✉ Avenida João XXI– Avenida da República ☎ 217 932 093 🚇 Campo Pequeno

GOLF

Lisbon Sports Club has a course at Belas, 10 miles north of Lisbon (☎ 214 321 474). Robert Trent Jones has designed courses at Quinta da Marinha, west of Cascais (☎ 214 860 100); Penha Longha, between Estoril and Sintra (☎ 219 249 011); and Tróia Golf Club, south of Lisbon (☎ 265 494 112).

SOCCER

Lisbon, like the rest of Portugal, is football-mad. The city's two main teams are Benfica and Sporting. Benfica is based at the giant Estádio da Luz and Sporting's home is the Estádio José Alvalade. Tickets for games (held on Sunday afternoon or evening) can be bought at the stadium, but for big games such as ones between the two local teams, or visits from F C Porto, it is best to try and buy tickets in advance from the booth in Praça dos Restauradores.
Benfica 🚇 E3 ☎ 217 263 663 🚇 Colégio Militar Luz
Sporting 🚇 G2 ☎ 217 514 098 🚇 Campo Grande

SWIMMING

In summer locals head for the beaches at Cascais, a former fishing village, the elegant old royal town Estoril, and Carcavelos. The towns' beaches stretch some 11 miles west of the city (though the town center ones are not recommended for swimming). They can be easily reached by regular direct trains from Cais do Sodré (some services change at Oeiras). The Guincho beach, which has a huge Atlantic swell, is known for its surfing, but is dangerous at night as people have been robbed at knife point. There are also several hotel pools, including the Lapa Palace (► 84), and public pools within the city limits.

TENNIS

Several major Lisbon hotels have tennis courts, some open to non-patrons. Otherwise, it is usually possible to play at one of the city's many public courts. Most accessible of these are in the Alvalade (Lisboa Racket Center) and at Estádio 1 de Maio. Contact the tourist office for details.
🚇 J3 ✉ Praça de Alvalade 🚇 Alvalade
🚇 J3–J4 ✉ Estádio 1 de Maio 🚇 Roma

Casino

Europe's largest casino, owned by the multimillionaire Stanley Ho, offers live shows along with fine dining in its world-famous Chinese restaurant, and world-class gambling facilities at its prime location in front of the sea at Estoril.
🚇 off map ☎ 214 667 700
🚇 Estoril on Cascais line from Cais do Sodré

Jogging

If you want a run during the day, you could head for the Parque Eduardo VII (avoid at night—reports of muggings), but better perhaps is the newly finished promenade linking the Doca de San to Marao to Belém. Pick up the train at either end
🚇 Alcântara/Belém 🚌 28

EXPENSIVE HOTELS

Prices

Approximate prices per night for a double room:

Expensive	over 20,000$00
Mid-Range	10–20,000$00
Budget	under 10,000$00

Reserving

Reserve a room well in advance if you plan to visit Lisbon over Easter or during mid-summer. At other times, it is safest to reserve, but some sort of accomodations can usually be found on arrival. The information desk at the main Portela Airport has details of day-to-day availability but cannot make reservations for you. The city's main tourist office in the Palácio Foz on the western side of Praça dos Restauradores operates a no-commission accommodations service (➤ 90).

AS JANELAS VERDES

An intimate 17-room hotel very similar in style to, and almost as popular as, the nearby York House (see below), situated in an 18th-century townhouse with spacious and sumptuously appointed rooms. Elegant, but the location means the front rooms can be noisy.

✚ G9 ✉ Rua das Janelas Verdes 47 ☎ 213 968 143; fax 213 968 144 🚌 40, 49, 60; tram 27

AVENIDA PALACE

This is the place to choose if you want a traditional hotel at the heart of the city. Built in 1842 and recently refurbished, it lies between the busy Rossio and Praça dos Restauradores, but the rooms away from the street are calm, comfortable, and spacious.

✚ H8; all ✉ Rua 1 de Dezembro 123 ☎ 213 460 151; fax 213 422 884 🚇 Rossio

LAPA PALACE

This 94-room hotel is one of Lisbon's newest and most expensive. It is in a 19th-century palace and a modern six-story block. Rooms are luxurious and the pool is set in the lovely garden.

✚ F8 ✉ Rua do Pau de Bandeira 4 ☎ 213 950 005; fax 213 950 665 🚌 13; tram 27

METROPOLE

An imposing and elegant building in the Rossio—central but also noisy. Air-conditioning and double glazing help.

✚ H8; bIII ✉ Praça Dom Pedro IV 30 ☎ 213 469 164; fax 213 469 166 🚇 Rossio

RITZ FOUR SEASONS

Lisbon's most famous deluxe hotel since it opened in the 1950s. All 310 rooms have their own balconies.

✚ H6 ✉ Rua Rodrigo do Fonseca 88 ☎ 213 811 400; fax 213 831 783 🚇 Marquês de Pombal 🚌 1, 2, 9, 11, 31, and all other Avenida da Liberdade services

SOFITEL LISBOA

One of the city's newest luxury options, with 163 rooms, this hotel is stylish and modern and appeals to business travelers as well as tourists.

✚ H7 ✉ Avenida da Liberdade 123 ☎ 213 228 300; fax 213 228 310 🚇 Avenida 🚌 1, 2, 9, 11, 31, and all other Avenida da Liberdade services

YORK HOUSE

Well west of the city center. However this is one of Lisbon's most popular hotels, with a lovely tree- and plant-filled courtyard, and 34 simple but tasteful rooms.

✚ G8 ✉ Rua das Janelas 32 ☎ 213 962 435; fax 213 972 793 🚌 27, 40, 49, 60; tram 25

SINTRA

PALÁCIO DE SETEAIS

A sumptuous 30-room hotel in a lovely 19th-century palace, with period furnishings. The views are all that you could wish of Sintra.

✚ Off map ✉ Rua Barbosa do Bocage 8, 2710 Sintra ☎ 219 233 200; fax 219 234 277 🚆 Sintra

MID-RANGE HOTELS

BRITÂNIA

A traditional, 30-room, hotel built in 1944 on a pleasant street one block east of the Avenida da Liberdade. Rooms were refurbished in 1995, but retain old-fashioned charm and art deco interior. Courteous service. Breakfast is the only meal served.

✚ H7 ✉ Rua Rodrigues Sampaio 17 ☎ 213 155 016; fax 213 155 021 🚇 Avenida 🚌 1, 2, 9, 11, 31, and all other Avenida da Liberdade services

CARLTON

The Carlton is modern but small and very prettily fitted out. It is close to the Gulbenkian—not central but with good transportation to the heart of Lisbon. Breakfast served but no restaurant.

✚ H5 ✉ Avenida Cibde de Valbom 56–62 ☎ 217 951 157; fax 217 951 166 🚇 S Sebastião 🚌 16, 18, 26, 42, 46, 56

CASA DE SÃO MAMEDE

This homey and pleasantly traditional pension is by the Jardim Botânico (► 56) on the northern fringes of the Bairro Alto. The 28 rooms are simple, but pleasantly furnished.

✚ G7 ✉ Rua da Escola Politécnica 159 ☎ 213 963 166; fax 213 951 896 🚇 Avenida 🚌 10, 20, 24, 29, 30

HOTEL JORGE

This 1960s building is conveniently situated just off the Avenida de Liberdade. Small rooms but some have nice balconies for breakfast and tea.

✚ G7–H7 ✉ Rua Mouzinho da Silveira 3 ☎ 213 562 525; fax 213 150 319 🚇 Marquês de Pombal 🚌 all Avenida de Liberdade services

MIRAPARQUE

An almost perfect mid-range friendly hotel on a quiet tree-lined street overlooking the Parque Eduardo VII and lovely old Pavilhão dos Desportos. Rooms are a little dated, but large, bright, and spotlessly clean. Serves good Portuguese food. The Metro is just a minute away.

✚ H6 ✉ Avenida Sidónio Pais 12 ☎ 213 524 286; fax 213 578 920 🚇 Parque

SENHORA DO MONTE

This lovely hilltop hotel in the Graça district, north of the Castelo, would be the first choice in its category if it were closer to the center. It has 28 very attractive rooms, some with balconies and air-conditioning, and a relaxed and amiable ambience. No restaurant, but breakfast is served.

✚ J7 ✉ Calcada do Monte 39 ☎ 218 866 002; fax 218 877 783 🚇 Martim Moniz 🚌 7, 8, 40; tram 12, 17,28, 35

SINTRA

CENTRAL

Right in the middle of town, looking towards the palace, the Central has 11 rooms with bath.

✚ Off map ✉ Largo Rainha D Amélia, Sintra-Vila ☎ 219 230 963 🚇 Sintra

Where to stay

Of the more expensive hotels, the older ones tend to be close to the Rossio, while the newer establishments lie to the north on, or just off, the Avenida da Liberdade. Other choice hotels lie in residential suburbs well away from the center, mostly in the west or northeast of the city. Most budget options are near the Rossio and in the Baixa, but these central locations are likely to be noisy unless you can secure an off-street room. Two of the city's most picturesque places to stay, the atmospheric Bairro Alto and Alfama districts, have relatively few hotels.

85

BUDGET ACCOMMODATIONS

Noise

Lisbon is notoriously noisy. Expensive hotels are not immune to the cacophony, but most have double-glazing and air-conditioning, which offer a measure of protection. Budget hotels are usually not so blessed, and may be near the Rossio, Baixa or Bairro Alto, three of the city's busier districts. Try to avoid rooms on the street, and check for bars or restaurants nearby which are likely to be open until the small hours.

Useful tips

If you are searching for inexpensive accommodations under your own steam, remember that many pensions are in buildings that look much more run down from the outside than they are inside. Many budget places are on the upper floors of blocks, so note the address carefully. In Lisbon a street number is often followed by the floor number: 74 – 3°, for example, means the property is at number 74 in the street and on the third floor. In Portugal this will be starting with the ground floor at street level, first floor one above street level, and so on.

HOTEL BORGES

A comfortable if unexceptional hotel worth considering for its fine location on the main street of the Chiado shopping district. Popular with tour groups, so reserve ahead.
➕ H8; alll ✉ Rua Garrett 108–10 ☎ 213 461 951; fax 213 426 617 🚇 Baixa-Chiado 🚋 tram 28

PENSÃO ARCO DA BANDEIRA

Welcoming clean pension located through the arch just off the southern corner of the Rossio. Some rooms are noisy, although all six have private bath.
➕ J8; blll ✉ Rua dos Sapateiros 226 – 4° ☎ 213 423 4 78 🚇 Baixa-Chiado

PENSÃO GALICIA

This pension is on the fourth floor of a block between the Baixa and Chiado districts, in the street immediately west of the Baixa's Rua Áurea (Rua do Ouro). Although all the rooms are smallish, some have balconies.
➕ J8; blll ✉ Rua do Crucifixio 50–54 ☎ 213 428 430 🚇 Baixa-Chiado

PENSÃO LONDRES

This friendly and efficient pension in an old townhouse is plusher than most in its price category. Rooms vary considerably; some on the fourth floor have views, so look first.
➕ H7 ✉ Rua Dom Pedro V 53 – 2° ☎ 213 462 203; fax 213 465 682 🚇 58, 100

PENSÃO NINHO DAS ÁGUIAS

Not all the rooms in the "Eagle's Nest" have views, but every guest can enjoy the panorama from the tower of this pension that is nicely situated in the Alfama beneath the Castelo.
➕ J8; bll ✉ Costa do Castelo 74 ☎ 218 864 070; no fax 🚋 Tram 12

PENSÃO SÃO JOÃO DE PRAÇA

An amiable pension in a nice townhouse, in a first-rate Alfama location, immediately east of the cathedral. Rooms, all on the second floor, are clean.
➕ J8; clll ✉ Rua São João da Praça 97 – 2° ☎ 218 862 591; fax 218 862 591 🚋 37; tram 28

POUSADA DE JUVENTUDE DE LISBOA

Lisbon's 200-bed youth hostel offers private double rooms as well as dormitory accommodations. The hostel is open all day, and there is no curfew.
➕ H6 ✉ Rua Andrade Corvo 46 ☎ 213 532 696; fax 213 537 541 🚇 Picoas

RESIDENCIAL CAMÕES

A perfect location in the Bairro Alto is the main selling point of this friendly first-floor *residencial*. Though small, the rooms are attractive, as are the communal areas. The more expensive rooms have balconies and/or private bathrooms.
➕ H8; alll ✉ Travessa do Poço da Cidade 38 – 2° ☎ 213 467 510; fax 213 464 058 🚇 Rossio/Baixa-Chiado 🚋 58, 100

LISBON
travel facts

ARRIVING & DEPARTING

Before you go
- U.S. and E.U. citizens require a passport or national identity card.
- Visas are usually required for nationals of other countries.
- U.S. visitors may remain for two months and E.U. for three months, before an extension visa is required.
- It is vital for all visitors to take out full health and travel insurance before traveling to Portugal.
- E.U. citizens are covered by reciprocal arrangements for medical expenses and are required to take an E111 form.

When to go
- The hottest and busiest months are July and August: the best months for a visit are April, May, June, September, and October.
- Hotels are especially busy from Easter to October.
- Despite the cooler, damper weather, winter can be delightful.

Arriving by air
- Internal and international flights use Lisbon's Portela Airport ⊞ J1 ☎ 218 413 500 or 218 413 700 for flight information, 4 miles or about 20 minutes' drive north of the city center. The approximate cost of a taxi from airport to city center is 2000$00; beware, airport taxis are notorious for overcharging.
- The Aero-Bus shuttle bus runs from outside the terminal every 20 minutes from 7AM to 9PM to the Rossio and city center.

Arriving by train
- International trains, and services from Porto, Coimbra, and other northern Portuguese towns, arrive at Santa Apolónia for general rail information.

Arriving by bus
- Some domestic and most international arrivals and departures are through the terminal off Praça Duque de Saldanha ⊞ H5–H6 ✉ Avenida Casal Ribeiro 18b ☎ 213 545 439 Ⓜ Saldanha. For services to Oporto and Algarve ☎ 218 879 324

Arriving by car
- Traffic jams, the lack of parking spaces, and the danger of theft make having a car in Lisbon a headache. You may wish to rent a car to go and see Sintra (➤ 20) though, as public transportation is irregular.
- If you do drive in the city, use a meter or official parking lot. Improperly parked cars are towed away. Contact your local PSP Police station for details of the nearest pound Ⓒ Daily 8–8
- Never leave possessions in your car.
- Car rental: Avis ☎ 800 201 002 (toll free) Europcar ☎ 219 407 790 Hertz ☎ 800 238 238 (toll free)

Customs regulations
- The limits for U.S. citizens and other non-E.U. visitors are 200 cigarettes or 100 small cigars or 50 cigars or 250g of tobacco; 1 liter of alcohol (over 22 percent alcohol); 2 liters of wine; 50g of perfume.
- E.U. nationals do not have to declare goods imported for their own personal use.

ESSENTIAL FACTS

Electricity
- Current is 220 volts AC (50 cycles), but is suitable for 240 volt appliances. Plugs are of the two-round-pin variety. U.S. visitors will require a convertor. These are available from specialist electrical stores in Lisbon.

Etiquette

- Do not wear shorts, mini skirts, or skimpy tops in churches, and do not intrude during services.
- Do not eat or drink in churches. Many churches forbid the use of flash and some ban photography altogether.
- Old-world courtesies are proffered and expected in Portugal. Always be respectful, especially toward the police and other people in authority.
- There are few non-smoking areas, but smoking is banned on public transportation (including boats).

Money matters

- The Portuguese currency is the escudo ($), which is made up of 100 centavos though never used.
- The "$" sign is placed between the escudos and the centavos. 200$50 means 200 escudos and 50 centavos.
- 1,000 escudos are known as a conto, written 1,000$00.
- Bank notes: 500$00, 1,000$00, 2,000$00, 5,000$00, and 10,000$00.
- Coins: 1$00, 5$00, 10$00, 20$00, 50$00, 100$00, and 200$00.
- On January 1, 1999, the euro became the official currency of Portugal and the escudo became a denomination of the euro. Escudo notes and coins continue to be legal tender during a transitional period. Euro bank notes and coins are likely to start to be introduced by January 1, 2002.
- Stores usually round prices up to the nearest 5$00.
- Foreign exchange bureaux (*cambios*) and banks offering exchange facilities are generally open Mon–Fri 8:30–3. You can also change money at the airport and Santa Apolónia railroad station (24-hour services); the main post

office (see below); and a few automatic exchange machines. Automatic Teller Machines (ATMs), or Multibanco, give credit card cash advances.

- Commission rates on travelers' checks are often high. Savings banks or building societies (*caixas*) may offer less expensive rates.

Opening times

- Stores: ⏰ Mon–Fri 9/9.30/10–12:30/1, 2:30/3–7/8. Many stores close for the weekend at 1PM on Saturday.
- Malls: may remain open very late, seven days a week.
- Banks: ⏰ Mon–Fri 8.30–2:45/3; some offer exchange facilities in the evening.
- Post offices: ⏰ Mon–Fri 8:30–6; larger branches occasionally open Sat 9–noon
- Restaurants: Lunch is usually served noon–3, dinner from about 7:30.
- Museums: ⏰ 10–12:30 and 2–6. Important museums may remain open all day. Most are closed on Mondays.
- Churches: ⏰ 7–noon and 4–7; some open only for early morning and evening services.

Places of worship

- Anglican: St. George's Church ✉ Jardim da Estrela, Rua de São Jorge 6 ⏰ Service Sun 11:45AM
- Baptist: Igreja Evangelica Baptista de Lisboa ☎ Rua Filipe Folque 36b ☎ 213 535 362
- Roman Catholic mass in English: Dominican Church of Corpo Santo ☎ Largo do Corpo Santo 32; ⏰ Service Sun 11AM
- Presbyterian: St. Andrew's Church of Scotland ☎ Rua Arriaga 13 ⏰ Service Sun 11AM
- Jewish: Shaare Tikau Synagogue ✉ Rua Alexandre Herculano 59 ☎ 213 881 592

Public holidays

- Jan 1: New Year's Day
  Good Friday
  Apr 25: Liberation Day
  May 1: May Day
  Corpus Christi (late May or early Jun)
  Jun 10: Camões Day
  Jun 13 : St. Anthony's Day
  Aug 15: Assumption
  Oct 5: Republic Day
  Nov 1: All Saints' Day
  Dec 1: Independence Day
  Dec 8: Immaculate Conception
  Dec 25: Christmas Day
- Shrove Tuesday is not a public holiday but functions as one.

Restrooms

- Public restrooms (*lavabos*) are few.
- Men's restrooms are marked *homens*, women's *senhoras*. *Quarto de banho* means "bathroom."
- You can usually use café and hotel restrooms without being a customer; otherwise use them at bus and railroad stations.
- To ask "where is the restroom," say *"onde ficam os lavabos?"*

Students and senior travelers

- Certain museums offer discounts to student and senior travelers. Discounted coach and rail travel are available on production of an under-26 youth card.

Time differences

- Lisbon observes the same time as Britain.
- Lisbon is 5 hours ahead of U.S. Eastern Standard Time and 8 hours ahead of Pacific Time.
- Summer time runs from the last Sunday in March to the last Sunday in September.

Tourist information

- Lisbon's main tourist office, or Turismo, is in the Palácio Foz in

Praça dos Restauradores ✚ H7; all ☎ 213 466 307 or 213 463 658 🕔 Mon–Sat 9–8, Sun 10–6
- There is also an information office at Portela Airport ✚ J1 ☎ 218 493 689 or 21 849 4323 🕔 Daily 6AM–2AM

Women travelers

- Women on their own should have few problems in Lisbon, but at night avoid parks, the Alfama, and areas around the stations and port.

PUBLIC TRANSPORTATION

- Public transportation information: Carris ☎ 213 632 044 (24 hours)
- Carris information kiosks are in Praça de Figueira in the Baixa and at the bottom of Santa Justa elevator in Rua Áurea (Rua do Ouro).

Buses, trams, and elevators

- Trams, or *eléctricos*, are one of Lisbon's highlights (► 19).
- Tickets for trams, elevators, and buses are interchangeable.
- A bus or tram stop is a *paragem*.
- The Elevador de Santa Justa runs from Rua Áurea (Rua do Ouro) in the Baixa to Largo do Carmo in the Bairro Alto.
- The Elevador da Glória funicular runs from Praça dos Restauradores to Rua São Pedro de Alcântara in the Bairro Alto. The Elevador da Bica goes from Rua de São Paulo to Largo Calhariz-Rua do Loreto.
- Buy tickets from the driver on a bus, tram, or elevator, or buy them for half the price from a kiosk.
- You can buy 2- and 4-unit tickets, or a book of 10 tickets (*módulos* or *caderneta*) that are less expensive.
- Tickets can be bought from machines (not from the driver) on the new large trams (notably the 15). You must have the right coins.
- Show pre-bought tickets and

passes to the driver or validate them in the machines on board.

- One-day or three-day bus and tram passes are available. Validate a pass the first time you use it: 24-hour or 72-hour validity starts from that moment.
- A Tourist Pass (*Passe Turístico*) gives unlimited travel for four days or seven days on buses, trams, subway, and elevators. It is available on production of a passport at the kiosks near the Santa Justa elevator (close to the Rossio), in Praça da Figueira, and the Restauradores Metro station.
- The Lisbon Tourist Pass (➤ 6) gives the best value if you are doing a lot of sightseeing.

Metro (subway)

- Buy tickets from vending machines (you need the right coins), or for slightly more from ticket booths at each station.
- Validate tickets in machines at station entrances, and retain them for the whole journey.
- A discounted ten-ticket *caderneta* and one- and seven-day Metro-only passes are available. Validate the pass on your first journey.
- Services run from 6AM until 1AM.
- Metro information ☎ 213 558 457

Taxis

- Lisbon's beige or black and green taxis are inexpensive and efficient, though hailing a cab can be difficult.
- Taxi ranks are located on the Rossio, Praça da Figueira, and elsewhere; or you can phone ☎ 218 155 061, 217 932 756 or 218 152 076
- A green light means the cab is taken.
- Fares are higher after 10PM, at weekends, and during public holidays. A charge of 300$00 may be added when the trunk is used for luggage over a designated size.

MEDIA & COMMUNICATIONS

Newspapers and magazines

- Lisbon has around ten local newspapers. Sports papers, women's magazines, and tabloids are the most widely read publications.
- The leading serious papers are the Lisbon-based *Diário de Notícias* and the Porto-based *Jornal de Notícias*.
- The main weekly news magazine is *Expresso*.
- You can usually buy the *International Herald Tribune*, *USA Today*, and European editions of the *Guardian* and *Financial Times* on the day of issue. Other foreign papers are sold the day after issue. The Rossio has several stands as does Praça dos Restauradores.

Postal services

- Post offices are *correios*. Mail boxes are red.
- Lisbon's main post office is at Praça do Comércio ✚ J8; bIV ☎ 213 463 231 🕐 Mon–Fri 8:30–6:30. Its poste restante service is at Rua do Arsenal 27 🕐 Mon–Fri 9–2
- There is another large office on Praça dos Restauradores ✚ H7; aII ✉ Rua Jardim do Regedor 50 🕐 Mon–Fri 8AM–8PM, Sat–Sun 9–6
- The airport has a 24-hour post office.
- Other post offices usually open Mon–Fri 8 or 9–6. Smaller offices may open 8 or 9–12:30 and 2:30–6. Main offices may open on Saturday morning.
- Buy stamps (*selos*) at post offices or stores displaying the sign "CTT Selos" or "Correio de Portugal Selos."
- Current prices for postcards and letters are 100$00 (E.U.), 98$00 (non-E.U. Europe), 140$00 (other foreign destinations).

- Air mail is *por avião*. The quickest express service is Correio Azul.

Telephones

- The Lisbon area code is 21 and must be dialed regardless of where you call from.
- Telecom pay phones are found in bars, cafés, tourist offices, and news dealers.
- Public coin phones accept 10, 20, 50, and 100 escudos coins.
- Public phones increasingly accept TLP or Credifone phone cards (from most post offices in 650$00, 1,300$00, and 1,900$00 denominations).
- Most post offices (➤ 91) have phone booths: tell the clerk where you want to call and pay when you have finished.
- Long-distance calls can be inconvenient to make from coin pay phones. It is best to use a Credifone or post office booth instead. There are no low-price periods for international calls from public telephones.
- English-speaking operator for reverse charge (collect) calls abroad, or dialing problems ☎ 098 (Europe and intercontinental). Information on international calls ☎ 099 National Directory ☎ 118

Television and radio

- Private and satellite channels show a plethora of game shows, sports, and Brazilian soap operas.
- Radio has many channels and a lot of advertising.

EMERGENCIES

Emergency phone numbers

- General emergencies ☎ 112
- Main police station ✚ H8; alll ⊠ Rua Capelo 13 ☎ 213 466 141 or tourist lice ☎ 213 14 3 324 ⏰ 24 hours

Report crime and theft here to make a claim on your travel insurance.
- Red Cross/Ambulance ☎ 219 421 111

Embassies

- Canada ✚ H7 ⊠ Avenida da Liberdade 144–156 – 4° ☎ 213 476 466 ⏰ Mon–Fri 8:30–12:30, 1–5 🚇 Avenida
- Germany ✚ H7 ⊠ Chancelaria 38, Campo Mártires da Pátria ☎ 218 810 210
- United Kingdom ✚ G7 ⊠ Rua de São Bernardo 33 ☎ 213 929 440 ⏰ Mon–Fri 10–12:30, 3–4:30 🚌 13, 27; tram 28
- United States ✚ F-G4 ⊠ Avenida das Forças Armadas ☎ 217 273 300 ⏰ Mon–Fri 8–noon, 1:30–5 🚇 Sete Rios/Entrecampos
- Australian and New Zealand nationals: consult British Embassy.

Lost property (lost and found)

- Police lost property office ✚ J6/7; bl ⊠ Rua Cidade Salazar Lote 180 R/C, Olivais ☎ 218 535 403 ⏰ Mon–Fri 9–noon, 2–6 🚌 10, 31
- Buses and trams ✚ H8; blll ⊠ Rua de Santa Justa 11 ⏰ Mon–Sat 3–7 ☎ 213 427 944 on the day, if not contact police (above) 🚇 Rossio
- Metro ✚ H7; all ⊠ Restauradores Metro station ☎ 213 427 707

Medical and dental treatment

- Consult your hotel for details of local doctors or call the British Hospital for advice (see below).
- British Hospital: most staff here speak English, but there is no casualty department ✚ F7/G7 ⊠ Rua Saraiva de Carvalho 49 ☎ 213 955 067 or 213 976 329 🚌 9; tram 25, 28
- For medication and prescriptions visit a pharmacy (*farmácia*). Details of 24-hour rota services are posted on pharmacy doors and in local newspapers. Normal opening is Mon–Fri 9–1, 2–7; Sat 9–1.

Sensible precautions

- Carry cash in a belt or pouch. Never carry valuables or wear expensive jewelry.
- Do not carry large amounts of cash. Use credit cards or travelers' checks.
- Be on your guard against pick-pockets on crowded buses, in markets, and in streets.
- Beware of strap-cutting thieves.
- Avoid the port, parks, railroad station districts, and the Alfama after dark.
- Water is safe to drink, but bottled water is widely available.

LANGUAGE

Portuguese is a Romance language, so a knowledge of French, Spanish, or Italian will help you decipher the written word. The spoken word is a different thing altogether. The pronunciation is difficult, at least at the outset. This said, most Portuguese welcome any attempt on the part of foreigners to wrestle with their vocabulary, though English is the second language taught in many Portuguese schools.

Pronunciation

- C is soft before *e* and *i*, but hard before *a*, *o*, and *u*.
- Ç is pronounced as an *s*, as in *almoço* (lunch).
- CH is soft: *chá* (tea) sounds like *sha*.
- E at the end of a word is silent unless it has an accent: *doze* (twelve) is pronounced *doz*.
- J is pronounced like the *s* in pleasure.
- G is pronounced like the *s* in pleasure before *e* and *i*, but is hard before *a*, *o*, or *u*.
- Q or QU is pronounced as a *k*.
- S at the end of a word or before a consonant is pronounced *sh*, as in *inglês* (English): otherwise the *s* sounds like the *s* in sit.
- X is also pronounced *sh*.
- ÃO sounds like a nasal *ow*, as in the English now.

Basics

yes/no	sim/não
please	por favour
thank you	obrigado (said by a man), obrigada (said by a woman)
hello	olá
goodbye	adeus
good morning	bom dia
good afternoon	boa tarde
good night	boa noite
excuse me	com licença
I'm sorry	desculpe
how much	quanto
where	onde
right/left	direita/esquerda
big/little	grande/pequeno
cheap	barato
expensive	caro
today	hoje
tomorrow	amanhã
yesterday	ontem
now	agora
later	mais tarde
open/closed	aberto/fechado
men	homens
women	senhoras
I don't understand	não compreendo
How much is it?	quanto custa?
At what time…?	a que horas?
Please help me	ajude-me por favor
Do you speak English?	fala Inglês?

1	um		9	nove
2	dois		10	dez
3	três		20	vinte
4	quatro		21	vinte e um
5	cinco		50	cinquenta
6	seis		100	cem
7	sete		101	cento e um
8	oito		1,000	mil

INDEX

INDEX

Citypack
Lisbon

Important note

Time inevitably brings changes, so always confirm prices, travel facts, and other perishable information when it matters. Although Fodor's cannot accept responsibility for errors, you can use this guide in the confidence that we have taken every care to ensure its accuracy.

Copyright   ©Automobile Association Developments Ltd 1997, 2001
Maps copyright ©Automobile Association Developments Ltd 1997, 2000
Fold-out map: © RV Reise- und Verkehrsverlag Munich · Stuttgart
                         © Cartography: GeoData

Published in the United Kingdom by AA Publishing

ISBN 0–679–00698–2
First edition

FODOR'S CITYPACK LISBON
          AUTHOR *Tim Jepson*
          UPDATED BY *Emma Rowley Ruas*
          CARTOGRAPHY *The Automobile Association*
                                    RV Reise- und Verkehrsverlag
          MANAGING EDITOR *Hilary Weston*
          COVER DESIGN *Tigist Getachew*
          COVER PICTURES *AA Picture Library*

Acknowledgments

The Automobile Association would like to thank the following photographers, libraries and associations for their assistance in the preparation of this book: Fundação Calouste Gulbenkian 34a, 34b (Centro de Arte Moderna); Instituto Português de Museus, Arquivo Nacional de Fotografia 26a (Museu Nacional de Arqueologia, José Pessoa), 51 (Museum of Chiado); Museum Arqueológico do Carmo 38; Museu de Marinha 25b; Pictures Colour Library Ltd 6/7, 18, 41a, 43; Spectrum Colour Library 41b.
All remaining pictures are held in the Association's own library (AA Photo Library) and were taken by Alex Kouprianoff with the exception of the following: M. Birkitt 6, 42b, 46, 59; D. Lyons 60a; P. Wilson 19, 24a.

Special sales

Color separation by Daylight Colour Art Pte Ltd, Singapore
Manufactured by Dai Nippon Printing Co. (Hong Kong) Ltd
10 9 8 7 6 5 4 3 2 1

Titles in the Citypack series